Excel

ADVANCED SKILLS

ENGLISH

YEAR 4

AGES 9–10

WRITING WORKBOOK

Get the Results You Want!

PASCAL PRESS

Laura Anderson

Reprinted 2017, 2019, 2020, 2022, 2023, 2025

ISBN 978 1 74125 404 4

Pascal Press
PO Box 250
Glebe NSW 2037
www.pascalpress.com.au

Publisher: Vivienne Joannou
Project editor: Rosemary Peers
Edited by Rosemary Peers
Series developer: Laura Anderson
Series consultant: Kristine Brown
Answers checked by Glenda Walsh
Proofread by Barbara Bessant
Cover and page design by DiZign Pty Ltd
Typeset by Kim Webber
Printed by Vivar Printing/Green Giant Press

Contents

To the student ... v

About this book ... vi

UNIT 1 Writing a recount ... 1
- Looking at recounts ... 1
- Student A: Arden's draft ... 2
- Writing the first draft ... 3
- Step-by-step improvement plan ... 4
- Writing the final draft ... 6
- Student B: Yan's draft ... 7
- Writing the first draft ... 8
- Step-by-step improvement plan ... 9
- Writing the final draft ... 11
- Your turn ... 12

UNIT 2 Writing a description of an animal ... 13
- Looking at descriptions ... 13
- Student A: Lucia's draft ... 14
- Writing the first draft ... 15
- Step-by-step improvement plan ... 16
- Writing the final draft ... 18
- Student B: Nhat's draft ... 19
- Writing the first draft ... 20
- Step-by-step improvement plan ... 21
- Writing the final draft ... 23
- Your turn ... 24

UNIT 3 Writing a sound poem ... 25
- Looking at poems ... 25
- Student A: Piero's draft ... 26
- Writing the first draft ... 27
- Step-by-step improvement plan ... 28
- Writing the final draft ... 30
- Student B: Emilia's draft ... 31
- Writing the first draft ... 32
- Step-by-step improvement plan ... 33
- Writing the final draft ... 35
- Your turn ... 36

UNIT 4 Writing to persuade—expositions ... 37
- Looking at expositions ... 37
- Student A: Eva's draft ... 38
- Writing the first draft ... 39
- Step-by-step improvement plan ... 40
- Writing the final draft ... 42
- Student B: Nicolas's draft ... 43
- Writing the first draft ... 44
- Step-by-step improvement plan ... 45
- Writing the final draft ... 47
- Your turn ... 48

UNIT 5 Writing an information report ... 49
- Looking at information reports ... 49
- Student A: Logan's draft ... 50
- Writing the first draft ... 51
- Step-by-step improvement plan ... 52
- Writing the final draft ... 54
- Student B: Eleanor's draft ... 55
- Writing the first draft ... 56
- Step-by-step improvement plan ... 57
- Writing the final draft ... 59
- Your turn ... 60

UNIT 6 **Writing a procedure** 61
Looking at procedures 61
Student A: Naomi's draft 62
Writing the first draft 63
Step-by-step improvement plan 64
Writing the final draft 66
Student B: Damian's draft 67
Writing the first draft 68
Step-by-step improvement plan 69
Writing the final draft 71
Your turn 72

UNIT 7 **Writing a narrative** 73
Looking at narratives 73
Student A: Musa's draft 74
Writing the first draft 75
Step-by-step improvement plan 76
Writing the final draft 78
Student B: Adina's draft 79
Writing the first draft 80
Step-by-step improvement plan 81
Writing the final draft 83
Your turn 84

UNIT 8 **Writing a discussion** 85
Looking at discussions 85
Student A: Ruby's draft 86
Writing the first draft 87
Step-by-step improvement plan 88
Writing the final draft 90
Student B: Aran's draft 91
Writing the first draft 92
Step-by-step improvement plan 93
Writing the final draft 95
Your turn 96

Answers 97

Word bank 105

To the student

This book will help you with your writing tasks, in English and in other subjects.

There are eight units altogether, each focusing on a different type of text. Some texts are imaginative, such as narratives and poems. Others are factual, such as reports and explanations.

Each unit contains an introduction that explains the purpose of the text and its special features. There are also examples of students' first drafts. These are followed by practice exercises that aim to improve the draft. Some of the exercises focus on the structure of the text while others focus on its language features. There is one example of a student's final draft. Make sure you read it carefully and answer the questions beside each paragraph.

At the end of the unit is a text in which words, sentences or paragraphs are missing. You should try to fill in the missing sections, using the step-by-step improvement exercises to help you. In the final activity, you are given a list of topics and you have to choose one to write about.

Most of the activities can be written in this book, but you will have to use your own paper for the final writing activity. I suggest you buy a notebook or folder for this. If you are not sure how to write something, use the sample texts and the checklists to help you.

It is best to work through the book from Unit 1 to the end. This will help you build on skills you have already learnt. However, if you are learning about a particular type of text in school, you could do that unit in the book. For example, if you are learning about information reports, you could do Unit 5.

It is important that you have a dictionary and a thesaurus handy as you work through the book, and that you ask for help if you need it. There is also a word bank of useful vocabulary at the end of the book to help you with your writing.

I hope you enjoy reading the texts and doing the activities.

Good luck!

Laura Anderson

About this book

This book consists of eight units, each covering a different type of text. Each unit contains two samples of students' first drafts, followed by exercises designed to help the students improve their drafts. There is one example of a final draft, which models the text for students. Students are then asked to complete a partially constructed final draft, and finally to construct a text independently. These last two activities allow students to put the knowledge they have acquired into practice.

The units are organised as follows:

An introduction to the type of text

This page looks at the features of the text. There are also short exercises to help students identify the type of text or its features.

Student A: Writing the first draft

These two pages focus on the planning and writing of the first draft. There is a comprehensive checklist that enables students to identify the features that have or have not been included in the draft, as well as other short exercises.

A step-by-step improvement plan

This section contains steps designed to help students improve the draft. Some of the steps focus on the structure of the text, while others focus on the language features.

Writing the final draft

The final draft is an example of a more advanced student's writing. It is accompanied by comments that point out the features of the text, as well as questions that ask students to identify some of the features.

Student B: Writing the first draft

The second half of the unit looks at another first draft, followed by a step-by-step improvement plan. Students are then asked to complete a partially constructed final draft.

Your turn

The final page of the unit contains a list of topics, from which students choose one to write about. There is a checklist to guide students in their writing. There is also a note directing students to a word bank at the back of the book where they can find useful vocabulary to help them with the writing task.

Word bank

At the end of the book is a word bank where students will find useful lists of words and phrases to help them complete their independent writing tasks.

Unit 1 Writing a recount

Looking at recounts

A **recount** is a retelling of events that have already happened, in the order in which they took place. When you write diary entries or historical reports, you are writing a recount.

The main **aim** of a recount is to **inform**, although it can also entertain.

A **recount** should have:

- an **orientation**, or introduction, that tells your reader **who** was involved, **what** happened and **where** and **when** it happened.
- a **sequence of events** in the order in which they took place.
- a **conclusion**, which can contain a **personal comment** about the events. For example: *We eventually got home at midnight.* **I was exhausted!**

Read the following **recount** and then answer the questions.

New | Reply | Delete | Archive | Junk | Sweep | Move to

From: Gina Hughes
Subject: Hello from the UK
Date: 6 January 2016
To: Samantha Jones sajones@firstnetwork.com.au

Hi Sam

I'm having a great time in the UK. I've met hundreds of aunts, uncles and cousins I've never seen before. Some of my cousins are my age.

We spent Christmas in Wales with my dad's family, and New Year in Scotland with my mum's family. One of my Scottish uncles is really funny. On New Year's Eve he wore a kilt, which is a kind of skirt for men, and played the bagpipes. My aunt says he does that every year.

I've enjoyed meeting my UK family, but it's freezing here and it rains a lot. I can't wait to get back to warm, sunny Australia.

See you soon. Love, Gina

1. Who has Gina met for the first time? ______________________________
2. Where is Gina? ______________________________
3. Why do you think Gina and her family have gone to this place?

   ____

   ____

4. In the last paragraph, underline the **comment** Gina makes about the weather in the UK.

Student A: Arden's draft

To learn more about each other's cultures and interests, Year 4 students each have to write a **recount** about the things they did on the weekend.

This is what Arden wrote on the worksheet his teacher gave him.

Weekend worksheet

Saturday morning Went shopping—boring, except for milkshake!	**Saturday afternoon** George came to my house—played computer games and watched TV. It was fun!	**Saturday night** Went to Aunt Maud's house for dinner. All my cousins were there—more fun!
Sunday morning Played soccer—our team won. Yay!	**Sunday afternoon** Grandma and Grandpa arrived. Had to help make the tabouli. Yum!	**Sunday night** Listened to my grandpa's stories—again!

1. Arden has included a number of **personal comments** about the things he did. Which comment tells us that:
   - **a** he likes tabouli? ______________________
   - **b** he is happy about something? ______________________
   - **c** he enjoyed spending time with his friend? ______________________
   - **d** he didn't enjoy going shopping? ______________________
   - **e** he has listened to Grandpa's stories many times? ______________________
   - **f** he enjoyed being with his relatives? ______________________

2. Use Arden's notes to help you complete these sentences.
   - **a** When George comes to my house, we usually ______________________

     ____
   - **b** I was happy when ______________________

     ____

     ____

Writing the first draft

Read Arden's **first draft** and then answer the questions.

My Weekend

On the weekend I did lots of different things with my family and friends. I spent time at home. I also went shopping, visited my cousins and played soccer.

On Saturday morning I went shopping with Mum and Dad. It was boring. I enjoyed the milkshake!

On Saturday afternoon my friend George came to my house. We played computer games and watched TV. It was fun.

On Saturday night we went to Aunt Maud's house for dinner. She's my dad's sister. They're Irish. We celebrate St Patrick's Day with my aunt's family. I played with my cousins. We had fun.

On Sunday morning I went to soccer. My team won. I was happy.

On Sunday afternoon Grandma and Grandpa came to our house. They're Lebanese. I helped make the tabouli.

On Sunday night we ate the tabouli. I listened to my grandpa's stories.

The weekend was over. It was time to go to bed.

1. A good **recount** should have the following features. Tick (✓) the ones that Arden has used.

   a an **orientation** (first paragraph) that tells us **who**, **what**, **when** and **where** ☐

   b **events** told in the **order** in which they happened ☐

   c **time connectives** to **link** the **events** (e.g. *on Saturday, later* or *then*) ☐

   d **interesting noun groups** to add detail to his sentences (e.g. *an ice-cold strawberry milkshake* or *an exciting game of soccer*) ☐

   e **past-tense verbs** (e.g. *went, was* or *helped*) ☐

   f **correct spelling** and **punctuation** ☐

   g a **conclusion** (last paragraph) containing a **personal comment** to round off the recount ☐

2. Arden has remembered to use **past-tense verbs** throughout his recount.

   Find and circle the past tense of:

   do spend come play eat

Step-by-step improvement plan

Before writing the final draft, Arden is going to do some exercises to find ways to improve his **recount**. Help him complete them.

Step 1: Link ideas with time connectives

Time connectives are **words** and **phrases** that **link events** in a recount.
For example: *First, In the morning, After that*
They help make your writing flow.

Arden needs to replace some of the time connectives in his draft with more interesting ones.

Replace the **time connectives** in bold with a different one from the box. Use each time connective once.

The next morning	After lunch	That night	In the afternoon	Later

1. On Saturday morning I went shopping with Mum and Dad.
2. **On Saturday afternoon** ______________________ my friend George came to my house.
3. **On Saturday night** ______________________ we went to Aunt Maud's house for dinner.
4. **On Sunday morning** ______________________ I went to soccer.
5. **On Sunday afternoon** ______________________ Grandma and Grandpa came to our house and we made tabouli.
6. **On Sunday night** ______________________ we ate the tabouli.

Step 2: Add interest with noun groups

Noun groups are groups of words that are built around a noun. They give the reader more **detail** about **who** or **what** is involved. They also make your writing more **interesting** to read.

The words that are built around the noun can be **articles**, (*a, an, the*), **pronouns** (*my, his, her, their*) or **adjectives** (*big, delicious, perfect*).
For example: **a large strawberry** *milkshake*

Use these **groups of words** to add detail to the nouns in bold in the sentences below. The pictures will help you choose the correct ones.

a very good

a brilliant

a young

two boring

my funny green

traditional Lebanese

1. On Saturday morning I spent ______________________ **hours** walking around the shops with my parents.
2. George and I watched ______________________ **program** on TV.
3. On St Patrick's Day I wear ____________________________________ **hat**.
4. The next morning we played soccer against ______________________ **team**.
5. My mum is Lebanese and when her parents come for dinner we always eat ______________________ **food**.
6. My grandpa likes to tell us how cheap everything was when he was ______________________ **man**.

Step 3: End with a good conclusion

The **conclusion** is the last paragraph. It should include a **personal comment** about the events in the recount.

1. Here are three **conclusions** for Arden's recount. Tick (✓) the one that contains a **personal comment**.

   a After my grandparents said goodbye to us, I went to my room and got my bag ready for school the next morning. Then I went to bed.

   b My grandparents left at about eight o'clock. After that I packed my bag for school the next day and got ready for bed. I really enjoyed spending time with my family and friends.

   c After my grandparents went home, I finished off a bit of homework and then I got ready for bed. I read my library book for a while, and then I switched off the light and went to sleep.

2. Use the **words** and **phrases** on the notes below to write a different **personal comment** for Arden's conclusion in question 1.

| it was | a busy weekend, | great fun! |
| I had | but | |

____

____

____

____

Writing the final draft

This is Arden's **final draft**. Read the comments about his **recount** on the left, and do the tasks on the right.

Comments

A clear **orientation** *tells* **who**, **what**, **when** *and* **where**.

Using **past-tense verbs** *shows that the events have already happened.*

Using **time connectives** *shows the* **order** *in which things happened.*

Using **noun groups** *gives more information about* **who** *or* **what** *is involved*

An interesting **conclusion** *contains a* **personal comment**.

My Weekend

On the weekend I did lots of different things with my family and friends. I spent time at home, but I also went shopping, visited my cousins and played soccer.

On Saturday morning I spent two boring hours walking around a shopping centre with Mum and Dad. Luckily Mum wanted to go to her favourite coffee shop, so I got to have a strawberry milkshake.

After lunch my best friend, George, came to my house. We played computer games for a while, and then we watched a brilliant program on TV.

That night we went to Aunt Maud's house for dinner. She's Irish, like my dad. I can't wait for 17 March when the Irish side of my family gets together at her house to celebrate St Patrick's Day! We all have to wear something green. I wear my funny green hat.

The next morning I played a soccer match. We were really happy when we won because the team we played against was very good.

In the afternoon Grandma and Grandpa came to visit. They stayed for dinner. They're Lebanese, like my mum, and whenever they come to our house, we have lots of traditional Lebanese food. One of our favourites is a type of salad called tabouli. It's an old family tradition that everyone helps to make the tabouli. My job was to wash the herbs and vegetables.

When dinner was over, I had to listen to Grandpa's stories. As usual, we heard all about how cheap things were when he was a young man and how far he had to walk to school every day.

Grandma and Grandpa left at about eight o'clock. After that I packed my bag for school the next day and got ready for bed. I really enjoyed spending time with my family and friends over the weekend.

Tasks

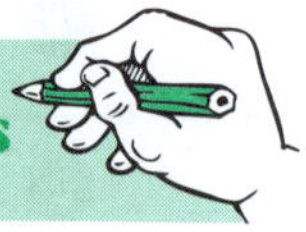

1. **Highlight** the **past tense** of *go*.
2. **Circle** the **adjective** that describes the milkshake.
3. **Underline** the **time connectives**.
4. **Circle** the **time connective**.
5. **Highlight** the **past tense** of *are*.
6. **Underline** the **noun groups** that are built around the nouns *food* and *tradition*.
7. **Highlight** the **time connective**.
8. **Underline** the **personal comment**.

Student B: Yan's draft

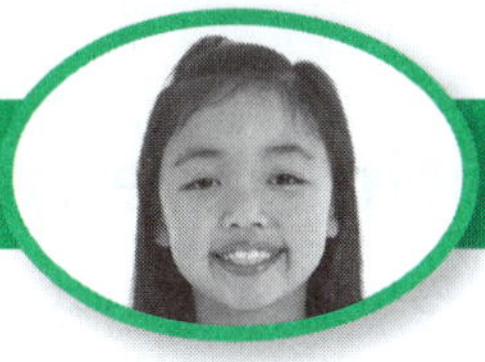

This is what Yan, another Year 4 student, did on the weekend.

My Weekend

Saturday morning Went shopping with Mum—started getting ready for Chinese New Year—exciting!	**Saturday afternoon** Helped Mum clean house—washed hair—tried on my new outfit	**Saturday night** Put up the final decorations
Sunday morning Put on my new outfit—lunch at restaurant—got lots of lucky money!	**Sunday afternoon** Went to New Year celebrations—brilliant!	**Sunday night** More celebrations—great fireworks

1 Write the **personal comment** Yan has made about:

a getting ready for Chinese New Year. ______________________

b the New Year celebrations. ______________________

2 Which **adjective** gives more information about:

a Yan's outfit? ______________________

b the decorations Yan put up? ______________________

c the money Yan got? ______________________

d the fireworks on Sunday night? ______________________

3 Use the following forms of the word *celebrate* to complete the sentences below.

celebrates celebrating celebrated celebrations

a Lots of other people were ______________________ Chinese New Year.

b For Chinese people, New Year is one of the biggest ______________________ of the year.

c Yan ______________________ New Year with her family and friends.

d Last year they ______________________ New Year in Hong Kong.

Writing the first draft

Read Yan's **first draft** and then answer the questions.

> ### Chinese New Year
>
> It was Chinese New Year on Sunday.
>
> On Saturday I went shopping with my mum. We had to get things for Chinese New Year. Then I helped Mum clean the house. I washed my hair and tried on my amazing new outfit. It looked good. I also helped decorate the house.
>
> On Sunday we had a delicious lunch with friends and family at my favourite restaurant. We gave each other lucky money. I got lots of money.
>
> Then we watched the parade. We saw acrobats, dancers, martial artists and other performers in the parade. I liked looking at all the different floats. I also liked the dragon and lion dances.
>
> The New Year celebrations ended with a fireworks display. It was amazing. Then we went home.

1. Which of these things has Yan remembered to include in her draft? Tick (✓) the correct answers.

   a an interesting **orientation** that tells **who**, **what**, **when** and **where** ☐

   b **events** in the **order** in which they happened ☐

   c **time connectives** to **link events** and make her **writing flow** ☐

   d interesting **noun groups** ☐

   e **past-tense verbs** ☐

   f **correct spelling** and **punctuation** ☐

   g a **personal comment** in her **conclusion** ☐

2. Yan has remembered to use **past-tense verbs** in her draft.

   Find and circle the **past tense** of:

   have　　wash　　give　　get　　see

3. Write down the word in the text that means:

   a a set of clothes. ____________________

   b a public procession. ____________________

   c people who entertain an audience. ____________________

Step-by-step improvement plan

Yan is also going to do some practice exercises to find ways to improve her **recount**. Help her complete them.

Step 1: Start with a clear orientation

The **orientation** is the first paragraph. It should tell your reader **who** was involved, **what** happened and **where** and **when** the events took place. It should also be interesting enough to grab your reader's attention.

Which **paragraph** would be the best beginning for Yan's recount?

A The weekend was one of the busiest and most exciting times of the year for me. It was Chinese New Year! ☐

B This weekend was Chinese New Year. On Sunday I went out for lunch and watched the celebrations. I had fun. ☐

C This weekend I helped my family prepare for Chinese New Year. We celebrated Chinese New Year on Sunday. ☐

Step 2: Link events with time connectives

Complete each sentence below with a **time connective** from the box. Use Yan's worksheet to help you sequence the events.

1. __________________ Mum and I went shopping.
2. __________________ I helped Mum clean the house.
3. __________________ I washed my hair and tried on my new outfit.
4. __________________ I helped put up the final decorations.
5. __________________ we had lunch with friends and family at a restaurant.
6. __________________ we went into the city to watch the New Year parade.
7. __________________ we went to a park to watch the fireworks display.
8. __________________ it was time to go to bed.

In the evening	The next day	Finally	On Saturday morning
After that	That night	After lunch	Then

Step 3: Add interest with noun groups

1. Yan has used the **noun groups** listed below in her draft.

   Underline the noun around which each group is built.

   The first one has been done for you.

   a my amazing new <u>outfit</u>

   b New Year celebrations

   c a delicious lunch

   d my favourite restaurant

   e all the different floats

   f a fireworks display

2. Now make these **noun groups** even more interesting by adding a word from the box to each group.

colourful	spectacular	talented

a many ____________________ acrobats

b the ____________________ floats

c a ____________________ fireworks display

Step 4: End with a good conclusion

Use the words and phrases on the notes to help Yan fill in the parts missing from this paragraph.

a spectacular fireworks display

I say that every year

celebrations

this year's celebrations

The New Year ________________ ended with ____________________________

____________________________, and then it was time to go home. I thought

____________________________________ were the best ever, but Mum says

____________________________________!

Writing the final draft

Yan has started writing the **final draft** of her **recount**. Help her complete it by filling in the missing sections, and then look in the answers section to compare what you have written with what Yan wrote.

Hint! Look at Yan's worksheet and practice exercises for ideas.

My Weekend

The weekend was one of the busiest and most exciting times of the year for me. It was Chinese New Year!

On Saturday morning I went shopping with Mum. We had to buy clothes and lots of other exciting things for the New Year celebrations.

After that, **(Write about what Yan did on Saturday afternoon and evening.)**

....

....

....

....

....

....

The next day we went to my favourite restaurant in the city where we met other members of our family and some special friends. My grandparents, aunts, uncles and cousins were there. It was so exciting! It's a tradition in our culture for the grownups to give children lucky money at New Year. They put the money in red envelopes because the Chinese consider red to be a lucky colour. I got lots of red envelopes and I'm feeling very rich.

After lunch we watched the New Year parade. We saw **(Write about the things Yan saw at the New Year parade.)**

....

....

....

....

....

....

....

The New Year celebrations ended with **(Write about the fireworks display and what Yan thought of the New Year celebrations.)**

....

....

....

....

Your turn

Write a **recount** of one to two pages on one of the following. Use your own paper for this activity.

Writing Checklist Make sure your recount includes: ✓

- an **orientation** that tells **who**, **what**, **when** and **where**. ☐
- a series **of events**, told in the order in which they happened. ☐
- **time connectives** to link events. ☐
- interesting **noun groups**. ☐
- a **conclusion** that contains a **personal comment**. ☐

Tip Use **Arden's final draft** on page 6 and **Yan's final draft** on page 11 to help you write your recount.

Go to WORD BANK page 105 for useful vocabulary

1. Write about the things you did last weekend. Use Arden and Yan's recounts as models.
2. Write about how you celebrated Australia Day this year or how you celebrated some other event that is part of your family's or cultural tradition, such as Diwali.
3. Write a recount that starts with the following:

   During the holidays I visited an interesting …

   The interesting place you visited can be in Australia or overseas. Tell about the things you saw and did there.
4. Imagine you are the boy or girl in these pictures. Write a recount about the events shown here.

Unit 2 Writing a description of an animal

Looking at descriptions

A **description** gives the reader a clear picture of a person, place, animal or thing.

It is usually part of another text. In a narrative, for example, it **helps tell the story**.

Sometimes a description can be a text on its own and then it should have:

- an interesting **introduction** that captures the reader's attention and tells **what** the description is about.
- **paragraphs** that **describe** the person, place, animal or thing.
- a **conclusion** that wraps up the description. This could be just a sentence or two.

1 Read the following short **description**.

> They are quite small and have furry coats. They can be white, brown, grey or black. Their eyes are on the sides of their heads and their long ears stand up straight. They have four short, powerful limbs that help them run very fast. They have short tails that look like balls of cotton wool.

You have probably guessed that this is a description of a rabbit.

In what type of text are you most likely to find this description?

a a narrative ☐ **b** an information report ☐ **c** a procedure ☐

2 Which passage gives a clearer **description** of the parrot?

a The parrot was sitting on a perch in its cage. It squawked loudly every time someone in the room laughed. Eventually its owner put it in another room. ☐

b The parrot has a strong, curved beak. It is a brightly coloured bird with strong limbs and claws. Some parrots can imitate human voices. ☐

Student A: Lucia's draft

The students in Lucia's Year 4 class each have to write a **description** of their favourite animal, without giving its name. Someone else in the class has to read the description and try to guess what it is.

Lucia's favourite animal is the giant panda. She starts by drawing and labelling it.

1. Which **adjectives** has Lucia used to describe the panda's coat, head and body?

2. Why would pandas find it difficult to escape if danger threatened?

3. What do you think it means if an animal is critically endangered?

Writing the first draft

This is Lucia's **first draft**. Read what she wrote and then answer the questions.

My Favourite Animal

My favourite animal is big, but not as big as an elephant.

It has a nice face. It has a large head. It has a heavy body. It has a short tail. Its colours are black and white. It is covered in fur. Its fur is thick and rough. It looks soft. It has black patches on its eyes. It can't run very fast. It has sharp claws. It can climb trees. It mainly eats bamboo. It can hold bamboo stems and leaves in its forepaws.

Can you guess what it is?

1. A good **description** should contain the following features. Tick (✓) the ones that Lucia has used.
   - **a** an **interesting introduction** that captures her reader's attention ☐
   - **b** a **paragraph** that **describes** the panda ☐
   - **c** **adjectives** that describe the panda (e.g. *thick, coarse*) ☐
   - **d** **present-tense verbs** (e.g. *is, has*) ☐
   - **e** **conjunctions** to **link phrases** and **clauses** and make her **writing flow** (e.g. *but, because*) ☐
   - **f** **correct spelling** and **punctuation** ☐
   - **g** a **conclusion** that wraps up her description ☐

2. Lucia has remembered to use **present-tense verbs** throughout her description. Which of these verbs show that an action is happening?

has ☐	is ☐	run ☐
are ☐	climb ☐	eats ☐

3. Look at Lucia's picture of the giant panda. What could she have said about the size of its ears?

____

____

Step-by-step improvement plan

Lucia wants to improve her draft. Help her find ways to do this by completing these practice exercises.

Step 1: Use interesting adjectives

Adjectives give **information** about nouns and pronouns.
For example: **thick** *fur*

Using interesting adjectives **adds colour** to your writing.

Replace each of the underlined **adjectives** below with a more interesting adjective from the box. Use each adjective once.

enormous	coarse	massive	cute	cuddly	stumpy

1. My favourite animal has a large ____________________ head.
2. It has a short ____________________ tail.
3. The black eye patches make its face look nice ____________________.
4. You'd like to hug it because it looks soft ____________________.
5. It is covered in thick, rough ____________________ fur.
6. It's a big animal, but not as big ____________________ as an elephant.

Step 2: Link phrases and clauses with conjunctions

A **phrase** is a group of words that does not make complete sense on its own.
For example: *a big head*

A phrase does not usually contain a verb.

A **clause** is a group of words that contains a **verb**.
For example: *The panda* ***has*** *a large head*
because it ***has*** *a large head.*

Conjunctions are words like *and, but* and *so*. They **link**:
- words and phrases in sentences.
- two or more clauses or sentences to make a single sentence.

Linking phrases and clauses with conjunctions makes our **writing flow**.

Here is a list of conjunctions:

although and because but if or so unless until when while yet

Complete each sentence below with a **conjunction** from the list. You may use the same conjunction more than once.

1. This animal has a massive head __________ a heavy body.
2. It can't run very fast, __________ it is a good climber.
3. This animal has short legs __________ a short tail.
4. This animal is critically endangered, __________ it has to be protected.
5. This animal's eyes __________ ears are black.
6. __________ this animal looks cute and cuddly, it can be dangerous.

Step 3: Use commas to make your writing easier to understand

Commas (,) are punctuation marks that show a **pause** in a sentence. We use them to:

- **separate phrases** and **clauses** in a sentence.
  For example: *It can't run fast, but it is a good climber.*
- **separate items in a list**.
  For example: *roots, stems and leaves*

Tip The conjunctions *and* and *or* are usually used instead of a comma to separate the last two items in the list.

Using commas correctly helps make the meaning of your sentences clear.

Fill in the **commas** in the following sentences.

1. Its eyes ears legs and shoulders are black.
2. It is covered in thick coarse fur.
3. If you ever see one of these animals it will most likely be in a zoo.
4. These animals will sleep anywhere but they like to lean back against something.
5. These animals have powerful teeth and jaws to help them chew the leaves stems and shoots of bamboo plants.
6. Because the nutritional level of bamboo is low these animals use as little energy as possible.

Writing the final draft

This is Lucia's **final draft**. Read the comments about her **description** on the left, and do the tasks on the right.

Comments

My Favourite Animal

An interesting **introduction** *captures the reader's attention.*

The animal I am going to describe is big, but not as enormous as an elephant. In the wild, it is found in forests in some mountain ranges in China.

1. **Underline** two **adjectives** that describe size.

Here are some clues that will help you form a picture of my animal in your mind.

2. **Highlight** the **future-tense verb**.

Using **interesting adjectives** *adds colour to the description.*

It has a heavy body and a massive head, and is covered in thick, coarse fur. Its eyes, ears, legs and shoulders are black, but the rest of its fur is white. It has black patches on its eyes that make its face look very cute.

3. **Circle** all the **commas**.

Using **conjunctions** *makes the writing flow.*

My favourite animal has a stumpy tail and short legs. It can't run very fast, but it is a good climber. Its sharp claws help it climb trees.

4. **Highlight** two **conjunctions**.

Using **commas** *correctly makes the meaning of your sentences clear.*

My animal eats mainly bamboo. It has powerful teeth and jaws to help it chew the leaves, stems and shoots of these plants. You often see pictures of it holding bamboo stems and leaves in its forepaws. Because the nutritional level of bamboo is low, my animal uses as little energy as possible.

5. **Circle** the **commas**.

Although it looks cute and cuddly, my animal can be dangerous. But don't worry—you'll probably never get close to it. It is critically endangered, so you are only likely to see it in a zoo.

6. **Underline** the **adjectives** that describe the animal's appearance.

Can you guess what my favourite animal is?

Tasks

Student B: Nhat's draft

Nhat is another student in Lucia's class. His favourite animal is the orangutan.

He also starts by drawing and labelling a picture of the animal.

Look at the picture of the orangutan's face.

1. How would you describe its eyes? ______________________________

____

____

2. How would you describe its nostrils? ______________________________

____

____

3. Which of these sentences best describes an orangutan? Look up the words in a dictionary if you're not sure what they mean.

It's a herbivore. ☐	It's a carnivore. ☐	It's an omnivore. ☐

Writing the first draft

This is Nhat's **first draft**. Read what he wrote and then answer the questions.

My Favourite Animal

My favourite animal is intelligent. It lives in forests. It is about seven times stronger than a human.

My animal is quite big. It has a thick body. It is covered in long hair. The hair is a reddish-brown colour. It has strong arms. Its arms are long. It has a big arm span. From fingertip to fingertip its arm span is about 2 metres. It has four fingers and a thumb. They are long. Its five toes are also long. Its fingers and toes are curved. This helps it climb trees. It sleeps in the trees. It makes a new nest every night. It can walk upright. It can also walk on all fours. It has short legs. Its legs are a bit curved. It doesn't have a tail.

It has a large mouth. It eats mainly forest fruits. It also likes insects and honey.

Can you guess what it is?

1. Which of these features has Nhat remembered to use in his draft? Tick (✓) the ones that he has used.
   - **a** an **interesting introduction** that gets the **reader's attention** ☐
   - **b** **paragraphs** that **describe** the orangutan ☐
   - **c** **adjectives** that **describe** the orangutan ☐
   - **d** **present-tense verbs** ☐
   - **e** **conjunctions** to **link phrases** and **clauses** ☐
   - **f** **correct spelling** and **punctuation** ☐
   - **g** a **conclusion** that wraps up his description ☐

2. Which **adjectives** has Nhat used to describe the orangutan's:
   - **a** hair? ____________________
   - **b** fingers and toes? ____________________

3. Why do you think the orangutan needs strong arms, fingers and toes?

____

____

____

Step-by-step improvement plan

Nhat is also going to do some practice exercises to find ways to improve his draft. Help him complete them.

Step 1: Use interesting adjectives

Replace the underlined **adjective** in each sentence below with a more interesting one from the list.

powerful	bowed	enormous
bulky	fresh	

1. My animal has a thick ________________ body.
2. My animal has strong ________________ arms.
3. It has a big ________________ arm span.
4. It makes a new ________________ nest every night.
5. When it stands upright, its legs are slightly bent ________________.

Step 2: Add detail with relative clauses

Reminder! A **clause** is a group of words that contains a **verb**.

A **main clause** makes complete sense on its own.
For example: *My animal lives in forests.*

A **relative clause** starts with a **relative pronoun**. It does not make complete sense on its own and depends on the main clause for its meaning.
For example: *My animal,* ***which is quite big****, lives in forests.*

Relative clauses help **add detail** to sentences.

The relative pronouns are *that, which, who, whom* and *whose*.

Complete the following sentences with a **relative pronoun** from the list. You do not need to use each one.

1. My animal, ____________ has long arms, is good at climbing trees.
2. Those of you ____________ have seen this animal in a zoo should easily guess what it is.

3. This animal, ______________ hands and fingers are curved, can easily grip onto branches.
4. This animal eats food ______________ it finds in the forest.
5. People ______________ work with these animals say they can be very affectionate.

Step 3: Link phrases and clauses with conjunctions

Join the phrases and clauses in the following sentences with a **conjunction** from the list. Use each conjunction once.

when	but	because
and	although	

1. My animal has a bulky body ______________ is quite big.
2. ______________ it has short, bowed legs, it can stand and walk upright.
3. It eats mainly fruit from the forest, ______________ it also eats insects and honey.
4. My animal needs long arms ______________ it spends a lot of time swinging from branches.
5. ______________ it stands, my animal's hands nearly touch the ground.

Step 4: Use commas to make your writing easier to understand

Fill in the missing **commas** in the following sentences.

1. My animal is covered in long reddish-brown hair.
2. This animal eats forest fruits leaves stems insects and honey.
3. It has long arms fingers and toes.
4. Every night before it goes to sleep it makes a fresh nest.
5. The animal's fingers and toes are curved so it is easily able to hang onto branches.

Writing the final draft

Nhat has started writing the **final draft** of his **description**. Complete it by filling in the missing sections, and then look in the answer section to compare what you have written with what Nhat wrote.

Hint! Look at the practice exercises for ideas.

My Favourite Animal

My favourite animal lives in forests. It is intelligent and is about seven times stronger than a human.

(Describe the animal's body and hair covering.)

....

....

....

....

My animal, which has long, powerful arms, is good at climbing trees. **(Tell about its long arm span and how far down its arms reach when it is standing.)**

....

....

....

....

My animal has four fingers and a thumb on each hand and five toes on each foot. Its fingers and toes are long and curved to help it grip on to branches when it climbs trees. It does not have a tail.

(Describe the animal's legs and how it walks.)

....

....

....

....

My animal sleeps in trees. Before it goes to sleep at night, it makes a fresh nest.

It eats food that it finds in the forest, like fruit, leaves, stems, bark, insects and honey.

Those of you who have seen my animal in a zoo should easily guess what it is.

Your turn

Write a **description** of about one page on one of the following. Use your own paper for this activity.

Writing Checklist Make sure your description has: ✓

- an interesting **introduction**. ☐
- **paragraphs** to describe the animal you are writing about. ☐
- interesting **adjectives** to describe the animal. ☐
- **conjunctions** and **relative pronouns** to link phrases and clauses. ☐
- **present-tense verbs**. ☐
- a **conclusion** that wraps up your description. ☐

Tip Use **Lucia's final draft** on page 18 and **Nhat's final draft** on page 23 to help you write your description.

Go to WORD BANK page 105 for useful vocabulary

1. Write a description of your favourite animal without mentioning its name. Use Lucia and Nhat's descriptions as models.
2. Use the photo and notes below to write a description of a koala.

quite small

cute face

curved, black nose

looks cuddly

sleeps a lot

eats eucalyptus leaves

round, fluffy ears

large head

stocky body

grey, white and brown fur

no tail

sharp, curved claws—ideal for climbing trees

Unit 3 Writing a sound poem

Looking at poems

Poems use words in imaginative ways to express **ideas** or to describe people or things. They are made to be spoken. The main difference between a poem and other kinds of texts is in the way it is set out.

A **poem**:

- is usually divided into **verses** or **stanzas**.
- often contains words that **rhyme**.
- often has a sense of **rhythm**, like a song.
- usually contains **descriptive words**.

This is the first stanza of Banjo Paterson's poem 'Frogs in Chorus'.

The chorus frogs in the big lagoon
Would sing their songs to the silvery moon.
Tenor singers were out of place,
For every frog was a double bass.
But never a human chorus yet
Could beat the accurate time they set.
The solo singer began the joke;
He sang, "As long as I live I'll croak,
  Croak, I'll croak,"
And the chorus followed him: "Croak, croak, croak!"

1. Which words in the poem **rhyme** with the following?

   a lagoon ____________ **b** bass ____________

   c set ____________ **d** joke ____________

2. The line *For every frog was a double bass* tells us that the frogs had:

   a soft voices. ☐ **b** sweet voices. ☐ **c** deep voices. ☐

Student A: Piero's draft

Piero's Year 4 class have been reading sound poems, like 'Frogs in Chorus'. Now they each have to write their own **sound poem**, using Roger McGough's poem 'The Sound Collector' as a model. Piero is going to write about the sounds people make.

The first thing Piero does is to look carefully at the first four stanzas of Roger McGough's poem.

1 A stranger called this morning
Dressed all in black and grey
Put every sound into a bag
And carried them away

2 The whistling of the kettle
The turning of the lock
The purring of the kitten
The ticking of the clock

3 The popping of the toaster
The crunching of the flakes
When you spread the marmalade
The scraping noise it makes

4 The hissing of the frying pan
The ticking of the grill
The bubbling of the bathtub
As it starts to fill

1. List three **sound words** in the second stanza.

   ______________ ______________ ______________

2. What **sound** do the flakes make? ______________

3. What hisses? ______________

4. Which words in the poem **rhyme** with these words?

   a grey ______________

   b lock ______________

   c flakes ______________

   d grill ______________

Writing the first draft

This is Piero's **first draft**. Read what he wrote and then answer the questions.

The Sounds People Make

Telling a secret
To my best friend
Screaming sounds someone makes
When they are scared

An audience that laughs
When it hears a joke
The noise my brother makes
When he drinks a coke

The sound of the choir
Singing a song
The students upset
When they can't do their work

The sound of happy people
Watching sport
The children all so happy
When it's time to go home

1. Roger McGough's **poem** contains the following features. Tick (✓) those that Piero has used.
   - **a** He has divided it into **verses** or **stanzas**. ☐
   - **b** He has used lots of **sound words**, like *hissing* and *purring*. ☐
   - **c** He has made the second and fourth lines in each stanza **rhyme**. ☐
2. What sound would someone make when drinking a coke?

   ____

3. Which two words in Piero's poem **rhyme**?

   ______________________ ______________________

4. Read Piero's poem out loud, clapping your hands in time to the words. Does it have a steady beat, or **rhythm**?

   Yes ☐ No ☐

Step-by-step improvement plan

Piero wants to improve his **sound poem**. He is going to do some exercises to find ways to do this. Help him complete the exercises.

Step 1: Add energy with onomatopoeia

Onomatopoeia (o-no-mat-o-pee-a) is where the **sound** of a word matches the sound of the action it is describing (e.g. *whoop* or *gurgle*).

Using onomatopoeia adds interest and energy to texts like narratives and poems.

Piero has not used enough onomatopoeic words in his draft so he is going to find some more.

These are some of the words he has found.

whispering	shrieking	chuckling	panting
squealing	chanting	puffing	muttering
grumbling	giggling	snorting	sobbing
humming	snuffling	groaning	whining

1. Write the words from the box under the correct heading.

Talking words	Shouting words	Crying words	Laughing words
______	______	______	______
______	______	______	______

Singing words	Gasping words	Snoring words	Moaning words
______	______	______	______
______	______	______	______

2. Add two more:
   - **a** talking words. ______ ______
   - **b** shouting words. ______ ______

3. Which of these are **sounds** that people usually make? Tick (✓) the correct answers.

burping ☐	jingling ☐	hiccupping ☐
fizzing ☐	sniffing ☐	munching ☐
bubbling ☐	yawning ☐	clapping ☐

Step 2: Add rhyming words

Rhyming words are words that have a similar end sound (e.g. gr*ey*, aw*ay*; *lock*, *clock*).

Rhyming words help give a poem its **rhythm**.

Tip! Rhyming words don't have to be spelt the same.

For example: *where, wear* *away, ballet* *release, police*

1. This is how Piero is going to start his poem:

Whispering a secret
In my best friend's ear

Circle the words below that **rhyme** with *ear*.

are	dear	fear	liar	near
air	here	fair	cheer	appear

2. Piero is going to start the third stanza like this:

The chanting of the choir
As they practise a song

Highlight the words that **rhyme** with *song*.

long	lounge	wrong	orange
sponge	along	thong	strong

3. This is how Piero is going to end his poem:

The happy squeals of children
When they hear the home-time bell.

Underline the words that **rhyme** with *bell*.

sell	ball	well	swell	peel	small
smell	tall	tell	yell	shell	feel

Writing the final draft

This is Piero's **final draft**. I am sure you will agree that now it has a better rhythm. Read the comments about his **poem** on the left, and do the tasks on the right.

Comments

Using **onomatopoeia** *adds interest and energy to the poem.*

Using **rhyming words** *helps give the poem rhythm.*

The Sounds People Make

The whispering of a secret
In my best friend's ear.
The shrieking of a little boy
Filled with fear.

The chuckling of the audience
When they hear a funny joke.
The slurping sound my brother makes
While drinking a coke.

The chanting of the choir
As they practise a song.
The groaning of the students
When they get an answer wrong.

The cheering of the crowd
When their team is doing well.
The happy squeals of children
When they hear the home-time bell.

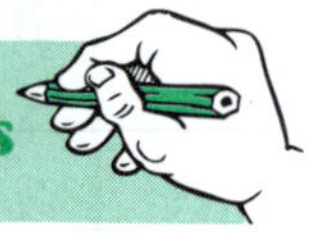

Tasks

1. **Underline** the words that **rhyme**.
2. **Highlight** the **onomatopoeic** words.
3. **Circle** the words that **rhyme**.
4. **Underline** the **onomatopoeic** words.

Student B: Emilia's draft

Emilia, another Year 4 student, is going to write a **poem** about the sounds animals make. She starts by looking at the last three stanzas of Roger McGough's poem.

5 The drumming of the raindrops
On the windowpane
When you do the washing-up
The gurgle of the drain

6 The crying of the baby
The squeaking of the chair
The swishing of the curtain
The creaking of the stair

7 A stranger called this morning
He didn't leave his name
Left us only silence
Life will never be the same

1. What makes a gurgling **sound**? ____________________

____

2. Which word matches the **sound** the curtains make?

____

3. Which **sounds** in the poem could animals make?

____________________ ____________________

4. Which **sound** in the poem would a musician normally make?

____

5. Which of these words means the same as *crying*? Tick (✓) the correct words.

bawling ☐ stammering ☐ wailing ☐

Writing the first draft

This is Emilia's **first draft**. Read it and then answer the questions.

The Sounds Animals Make

The geese in the yard
The dogs are barking
The cats are meowing
I can hear the frogs

The seagulls are crying
The hens are laying eggs
The cows are in the paddock
The pigs go oink oink

Sheep make a funny noise
Listen to the bees
A lion makes a scary sound
Birds like to sing

Ducks go quack quack
There goes a little mouse
The owl goes hoot hoot
Trying to catch the mouse

1. Tick (✓) the things Emilia has remembered to do in her poem.
   - **a** divide the poem into **verses** or **stanzas** ☐
   - **b** use lots of **sound words** ☐
   - **c** make the second and fourth lines in each stanza **rhyme**. ☐
2. **a** List all the **sound words** that Emilia has used. ______________________

   ____

   ____

   b For which animals has Emilia not used words that match the **sounds** they make?

   ____

   ____

   ____

Step-by-step improvement plan

Emilia is also going to do some exercises to find ways to improve her **sound poem**. Help her complete them.

Step 1: Add energy with onomatopoeia

Emilia has used lots of onomatopoeic words in her draft, but she could add more.

1. Match the animal to the **sound** it makes.

Animal	Sound
geese	buzzing
lion	clucking
frogs	baaing
mouse	squawking
hens	roaring
cows	cackling
birds	croaking
sheep	mooing
seagulls	twittering
bees	squeaking

2. Choose other **sounds** that dogs, birds and bees make from the lists below.

Dogs		Birds		Bees	
groaning	☐	cheeping	☐	humming	☐
growling	☐	bubbling	☐	screeching	☐
howling	☐	sighing	☐	droning	☐
snarling	☐	tweeting	☐	murmuring	☐
purring	☐	chirping	☐	swishing	☐
woofing	☐	cooing	☐	whining	☐

3. Circle the correct **sound** in brackets to complete each sentence.
   - **a** The snake was (hissing, roaring) angrily.
   - **b** The monkeys are (trumpeting, chattering) in the trees.
   - **c** The mosquito was (grunting, whining) around my head.

Step 2: Add rhyming words

Emilia is looking for words that rhyme with some of the animal names in her poem.

1. Circle the words that **rhyme** with the name of the animal at the top of each list.

dogs
socks frogs rocks
logs jogs clocks
fogs

cats
bats mates mats
plaits plates rats
gnats

seagull
dull glue rule
hull skull full
bull

hens
jeans pens sense
wrens tens tense
dens

cows
meows flows bows
blows rows slows
crows

bees
sneeze knees trees
peace fleece geese

ducks
lucky sucks clucks
flocks trucks fox

mouse
house hose those
grouse louse toes

2. Find words in the box to make the following lines **rhyme**.

a The birds are singing
The cow bells are ____________

b The howling of the hounds
And many other ____________

c The soft bleats of the lambs
The loud bleats of the ____________

songs sounds rams ringing ewes lowing

3. Cross out the words that **do not rhyme** with the word at the top of each list.

songs
clangs thongs
wrongs sons gongs
sings

ewes
mews two
sweets fuse accuse
stews

lowing
sowing crowing
browning flowering
glowing knowing

Writing the final draft

Emilia has started writing the **final draft** of her **poem**. Help her complete it, and then look in the answers section to compare what you have written with what Emilia wrote.

Hint! Use the practice exercises to help you.

The Sounds Animals Make

Meow meow

The cackling of the geese
The barking of the ______________
The meowing of the cats
The ______________ of the ______________

Croak croak

Squawk squawk

The squawking of the seagulls
The clucking of the ______________
The mooing of the ______________
Grunting ______________ inside their pens

Moo moo

Oink oink

The baaing of the sheep
The buzzing of the ______________
The ______________ of the lions
______________ cheeping in the ______________

Buzz buzz

The quacking of the ______________
The ______________ of a mouse
The ______________ of an owl
As it flies above our ______________

Quack quack

Hoot hoot

Your turn

Write a **sound poem** of four stanzas on one of the following. Use your own paper for this activity.

Writing Checklist Make sure your poem contains: ✓

- lots of **onomatopoeic words**. ☐
- words at the end of lines 2 and 4 in each stanza that **rhyme** with each other. ☐

Tip Use **Piero's final draft** on page 30 and **Emilia's final draft** on page 35 to help you write your poem.

Go to WORD BANK page 105 for useful vocabulary

1. Write a poem entitled 'The Sounds of the Playground'.
2. Write a poem about the sounds you hear at the beach or in the city.
3. Use the words below to write your own sound poem.

vrooming rattling cracking tinkling

smashing popping fizzing booming

zapping clanging whooshing whirring

4. Write a poem about the sounds the people in this picture might be hearing.

Unit 4 Writing to persuade—expositions

Looking at expositions

An **exposition** aims to **persuade** people that a certain **opinion** or **point of view** is the right one.

We have all tried to persuade someone to do something or agree with us at some point in our lives. However, people also make speeches and write letters, articles and blogs to try to persuade others to their point of view.

An **exposition** should have:

- an **opening paragraph** that states your main **opinion**.
  For example: *I believe people who live in the city should use buses and trains instead of cars.*
- **arguments** or reasons for your opinion.
  For example: *Firstly, more people can fit on a bus or train, so there wouldn't be as many vehicles on the roads.*
- a **conclusion** that **repeats** your main opinion and **refers back** briefly to your arguments.
  For example: *As you can see from the reasons I've given, it would be much better for the environment if people stopped using their cars in the city.*

1 Which of the following two sentences expresses an **opinion**?

a I definitely think we spend too much time at school. ☐

b Altogether we spend thirty hours at school every week. ☐

2 Which child is trying to persuade their father to let them watch a TV program?

a Dad, what time does that new program about robots start? ☐

b Watching that program will really help me with my science project, Dad. ☐

Student A: Eva's draft

Eva's Year 4 teacher has shown his students six items that are commonly used in a classroom.

They each have to choose the item they think is the most useful to have in a school bag. They then have to present reasons for their choice in a **blog** to be posted on the class website.

Eva has chosen the rubber band. She starts by briefly listing her reasons.

Reasons:	1 a hair tie 2 can hold things together 3 a reminder
Supporting details:	helps you remember to get forms signed keeps hair out of your face stops you losing papers or posters helps keep you cool on a hot day can wear it on your wrist makes it easier to carry things

Complete the table below with the correct details from Eva's notes.

Reason	Supporting details
1 a hair tie	
2 can hold things together	
3 a reminder	

Writing the first draft

This is Eva's **first draft**. Read what she wrote and then answer the questions.

Why I Would Choose the Rubber Band

I would definitely always keep a rubber band in my school bag. I think it is the most useful item. This is why.

It makes a good hair tie. You can tie back long hair. It stops it getting in your face. That's good when you're playing sport. It makes you feel cooler on a hot day.

A rubber band is good for wrapping around things. You can wrap it around posters and papers. It keeps them together. It makes them easier to carry. You won't lose them.

Rubber bands make great reminders. You can wear them on your wrist to remind you to do things.

I believe the rubber band is definitely the most useful.

1. A good **exposition** should contain the following features. Tick (✓) the ones that Eva has used.

   a an **introduction** that states her main **opinion** ☐

   b **reasons** for her opinion ☐

   c **details** to support her reasons ☐

   d **thinking** and **feeling verbs** (e.g. *believe, think*) ☐

   e **present-tense verbs** (e.g. *is, have*) ☐

   f **connectives** to link her **arguments** (e.g. *Firstly, In addition*) ☐

   g **conjunctions** to link words, phrases and sentences (e.g. *and, but, or*) ☐

   h a separate **paragraph** for each argument ☐

   i **correct spelling** and **punctuation** ☐

   j a **conclusion** that **repeats** her main opinion AND **refers back** to her arguments. ☐

2. Underline the two thinking and feeling **verbs** that Eva has used in her draft.

3. Which word has Eva used twice to show how strongly she believes that the rubber band is the most useful item? ____________________

4. What other uses can you think of for a rubber band? List at least two things.

   ____

   ____

Step-by-step improvement plan

Eva is going to do some practice exercises to find ways to improve her draft. Help her complete them.

Step 1: Start with a strong introduction

The **introduction** is the first paragraph. It should state the main **opinion**, but it should also be **interesting**.

Which of these sentences could Eva use in her **introduction** to make it stronger?

1. I don't have enough space to list all the different ways you can use a rubber band at school, so I'm only going to mention three ways. ☐

2. I have heaps of rubber bands. They are really fun to play with. I think everybody should have a good supply of rubber bands. ☐

Step 2: Link arguments with connectives

Connectives are words and phrases that link ideas in a text. They help us organise our writing and make it flow.

Use the **connectives** from the box to complete this passage. Use each connective once.

Tip Read through the passage before choosing your connectives. Start with *Firstly*.

in addition	firstly	secondly	finally	also	for example

______________________, a rubber band makes an excellent hair tie.

______________________, rubber bands are cheaper than normal hair ties, so they

______________________ save you money.

______________________, a rubber band is useful for wrapping around things.

______________________, it is perfect for holding together posters and papers.

______________________, rubber bands make great reminders.

Step 3: Use conjunctions to link ideas

In Unit 2 you learnt that **conjunctions** are words like *and, but* and *so*. They **link**:
- words and phrases in sentences.
- two or more clauses to make a single sentence.

Conjunctions make our **writing flow** and let us add **detail** to sentences.

Reminder! Here is a list of conjunctions: *although, and, if, but, or, so, yet, because, unless, until, when, while.*

Complete each sentence below with a **conjunction** from the list. Try to use a different conjunction each time.

1. Rubber bands are handy ____________ you have to tie your hair back.
2. Girls with long hair have to tie their hair back ________________ they play sport.
3. Girls tie their hair back in summer ________________ it makes them feel cooler.
4. I slip a rubber band on my wrist ________________ I don't forget to do things.
5. The other items can also come in handy, ________________ I believe the rubber band is the most useful.

Step 4: End with a strong conclusion

The **conclusion** is the final paragraph. It should **repeat** your main opinion and **refer back** to your arguments.

Eva is not happy with her conclusion, so she has practised writing three more.

Which one repeats her opinion and refers back to her arguments?

1. I love using rubber bands. I have lots and lots of them. They are great. I am sure everyone agrees with me. ☐

2. Rubber bands are much better than paperclips, pencils, pens or any of those other items. I use rubber bands all the time. ☐

3. I know that the other items can also come in handy, but I am sure that my arguments have convinced you that the rubber band is the most useful. ☐

Writing the final draft

This is Eva's **final draft**. Read the comments on the left, and do the tasks on the right.

Comments

Tasks

Why I Would Choose the Rubber Band

Starting with a strong ***introduction*** *gets your reader's attention.*

I definitely think the rubber band is the most useful item to have in your school bag. I don't have enough space to list all the different ways it can be used, so I am only going to mention three of them.

1. **Underline** Eva's **opinion**.

Using ***connectives*** *to link your arguments makes your writing flow.*

Firstly, a rubber band makes an excellent hair tie. If you have long hair like me, there are always times when you have to tie your hair back, such as when you are playing sport or just want to feel cooler on a hot day. In addition, rubber bands are cheaper than normal hair ties, so they can save you money.

2. **Highlight** three **conjunctions**.

Using a separate ***paragraph*** *for each argument makes your text easier to read.*

Secondly, a rubber band is useful for wrapping around things. For example, if you have posters or papers to take to or from school, a rubber band is perfect for holding them together. This way they are easier to carry and you are less likely to lose them.

3. **Underline** two **connectives**.

Giving ***examples*** *adds weight to your arguments.*

Finally, rubber bands make great reminders. For instance, if you have to give your parents a form to sign for school, slipping a rubber band around your wrist will remind you about it.

4. **Underline** the **phrase** that tells **how** you can use a rubber band to remind you about something.

Ending with a ***conclusion*** *that repeats the opinion and refers back to the arguments wraps up your exposition.*

I know that the other items can also come in handy, but I am sure that my arguments have convinced you that the rubber band is the most useful.

5. **Highlight** the **conjunction**.

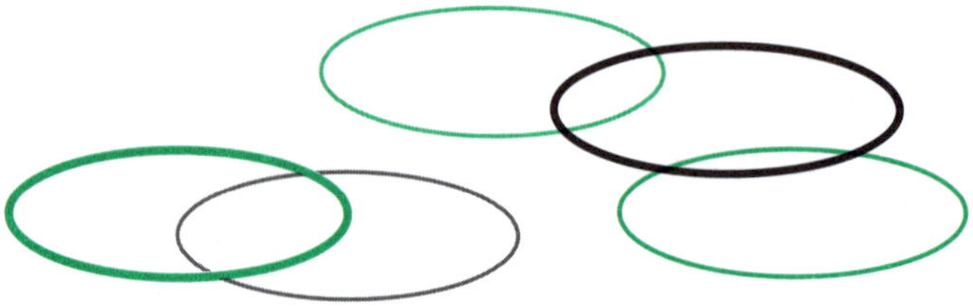

Student B: Nicolas's draft

Nicolas, another Year 4 student, thinks the paperclip is the most useful of the six items.

He also starts by jotting down some ideas.

Reasons:

1 holds things together
2 can bend it into different shapes
3 repairs things

Supporting details:

fixes a book
turns into a hook
displays photos and cards
makes a sculpture
sorts notes and papers
unclogs plastic containers
seals plastic bags

Help Nicolas organise his ideas by filling in the argument that goes with the supporting details.

Reason	Supporting details
1	fixes a book unclogs plastic containers
2	seals plastic bags sorts notes and papers displays photos and cards
3	makes a sculpture turns into a hook

Writing the first draft

This is Nicolas's **first draft**. Read what he wrote and then answer the questions.

Why I Would Choose the Paperclip

I would definitely choose a paperclip to have in my school bag. Actually, I would have quite a few of them.

You can use them to fix things. Sometimes the pages of a book come apart. You can use a paperclip to put them back together. Sometimes the glue in a glue bottle clogs up the little hole at the top. You can push the end of a paperclip through it to unclog it.

You can use paperclips to hold things together. You can clip papers or notes together. You can seal a plastic bag with a paperclip. You can use paperclips to attach photos and cards to a piece of string to make a classroom display.

You can bend paperclips into different shapes. You can use them in craft lessons to make things such as hooks or sculptures.

The paperclip is definitely the most useful item.

1. Which of these features has Nicolas remembered to use in his draft? Tick (✓) the ones that Nicolas has used.
   - **a** an **introduction** that states his **opinion** in an interesting way ☐
   - **b** **reasons** for his opinion ☐
   - **c** **details** to support his reasons ☐
   - **d** **thinking** and **feeling verbs** ☐
   - **e** **present-tense verbs** ☐
   - **f** **connectives** to link his **arguments** ☐
   - **g** **conjunctions** to link words, phrases and sentences ☐
   - **h** a separate **paragraph** for each argument ☐
   - **i** **correct spelling** and **punctuation** ☐
   - **j** a **conclusion** that **repeats** his opinion AND **refers back** to his arguments. ☐

2. What other uses can you think of for a paperclip? List at least two things.

____

____

3. Which do you think is more useful: a rubber band or a paperclip? Give a reason for your choice. ______________________

____

____

Step-by-step improvement plan

Nicolas also needs to work on his draft to make it more interesting. Help him complete these exercises to find ways to do this.

Step 1: Start with a strong introduction.

This is what Nicolas has written so far for his **introduction**.

I would definitely choose a paperclip to have in my school bag. Actually, I would have quite a few of them.

Help him choose one of the sentences below to add to his **introduction**.

1. They are made of metal or plastic and are sometimes very colourful. ☐
2. I think the paperclip is by far the most useful of the six items, for the following reasons. ☐
3. I have hundreds of them in my desk drawer at home. ☐

Step 2: Use conjunctions to link ideas

Write on the line the **conjunction** in brackets that correctly completes each sentence.

1. (So, If) __________ the pages of your book come loose, a paperclip will keep them in place.
2. A paperclip will keep the pages of your book together (until, when) __________ you can get the book fixed.
3. Paperclips help you keep your notes or papers organised, (but, and) __________ they are perfect for sealing plastic bags.
4. You can use paperclips to attach photos, cards (or, nor) __________ anything else to a piece of string.
5. You can bend paperclips into different shapes, (yet, so) __________ you can be very creative with them.

Step 3: Link arguments with connectives

Nicolas's **exposition** will flow better if he uses **connectives** to link his arguments.

Complete the following passage with **connectives** from the box. Use each connective once.

Hint! You have been given the first letter of some of the connectives to help you.

also	for example	secondly	for instance	finally	in addition	firstly

F ______________, a paperclip is handy for fixing things. F ______________, if the pages of your book come loose, a paperclip will keep them in place. It can ______________ be turned into a little pin that can be used for all sorts of things. ______________, paperclips are good for holding things together. They help you keep your notes or papers together. I ______________, you can use them to attach photos to a piece of string.

______________, you can bend a paperclip into different shapes, so you can be very creative with it; f ______________, you can turn it into a hook or sculpture.

Step 4: End with a strong conclusion

Nicolas wants to end his **blog** on a strong note. Help him write a good **conclusion**, using the words and phrases on the notes.

Tip! Remember to use **conjunctions** where necessary!

only given	a few examples	different ways	use a paperclip
However	sure my arguments	have convinced	most useful

____

____

____

____

____

____

Writing the final draft

Nicolas has started writing the **final draft** of his **blog**. Help him complete it by filling in the missing sections, and then look in the answers section to compare what you have written with what he wrote.

Hint! Look at his practice exercises for ideas.

Why I Would Choose the Paperclip

I would definitely choose a paperclip to have in my school bag. Actually, I would have quite a few of them. I think the paperclip is by far the most useful of the six items, for the following reasons.

Firstly, a paperclip is handy for fixing things. For example, if the pages of your book come loose, a paperclip will keep them in place until you can get the book fixed. A paperclip can also be turned into a little pin that can be used for all sorts of things, like unclogging the little opening at the top of a glue bottle.

Secondly, **(Write about how you can use it to hold things together.)**

Finally, you can bend a paperclip into different shapes, so you can be very creative with it; for instance, you can turn it into a hook or sculpture.

(Write the conclusion.)

Your turn

Write an **exposition** of about a page on one of the following. Use your own paper for this activity.

Writing Checklist Make sure your exposition includes: ✓

- an opening paragraph in which you **state** your **opinion**. ☐
- **reasons** for your opinion. ☐
- **details** to support your reasons. ☐
- **thinking** and **feeling verbs**. ☐
- **present-tense verbs**. ☐
- **connectives** to link **arguments** and ideas. ☐
- **conjunctions** to link words, phrases and sentences. ☐
- **paragraphs** to organise your writing. ☐
- a **conclusion** that **repeats** the opinion and **refers back** briefly to the arguments. ☐

Tip Use **Eva's final draft** on page 42 and **Nicolas's final draft** on page 47 to help you write your exposition.

Go to WORD BANK page 105 for useful vocabulary

1. Which do you think is more useful: a pencil or a ballpoint pen? Give reasons for your choice.
2. For your birthday, would you rather be given a big party or money? Give reasons for your choice.

Unit 5 Writing an information report

Looking at information reports

An **information report** provides facts and information about a subject.

You will often have to write **information reports**, especially for subjects like history and geography. For example, you might have to write about:

- plants or animals (e.g. eucalyptus trees or wombats).
- technology (e.g. computers or motor cars).
- people, countries and cultures (e.g. Indigenous Australians or Egypt).

An **information report** should have:

- an **introduction** that includes a **short definition** or **description** of the subject.
- **paragraphs** that give factual information (not opinions) about your subject. These paragraphs may be organised under **subheadings**.
- a **conclusion** that rounds off the report.

Hint! We often use **diagrams** and **charts** in information reports.

Read the short **information report** below and then answer the questions.

Egypt

Egypt is a country in North Africa. It gets very little rain and is mainly desert.

If it wasn't for the Nile River, the whole of Egypt would be desert. Every year rains to the south of Egypt cause the Nile to overflow its banks. The soil that is left behind after each flood is very fertile and the people are able to grow crops.

Egypt is home to a wide variety of animals, such as crocodiles, snakes, cheetahs and hyenas.

Egypt has a large population. Most of the people live close to the Nile River. The capital, Cairo, is one of the biggest cities in the world.

An interesting fact about Egypt is that the Great Pyramid of Giza, on the west bank of the Nile River, is the oldest of the seven wonders of the ancient world.

1. What does the **introduction** tell us about Egypt? Tick (✓) the correct answers.

   a where it is ☐ **b** how many people live there ☐

   c how big it is ☐ **d** what it looks like ☐

2. Where would you expect to find crocodiles in Egypt? ______________________

3. If you were using subheadings, which one would you choose for paragraph 2?

   a The desert ☐ **b** The people of Egypt ☐ **c** The Nile River ☐

Student A: Logan's draft

Logan's Year 4 class are learning in geography about South America. They have to research a South American country and write an **information report** about it. Logan is going to write about Chile.

He is using the following poster to help him.

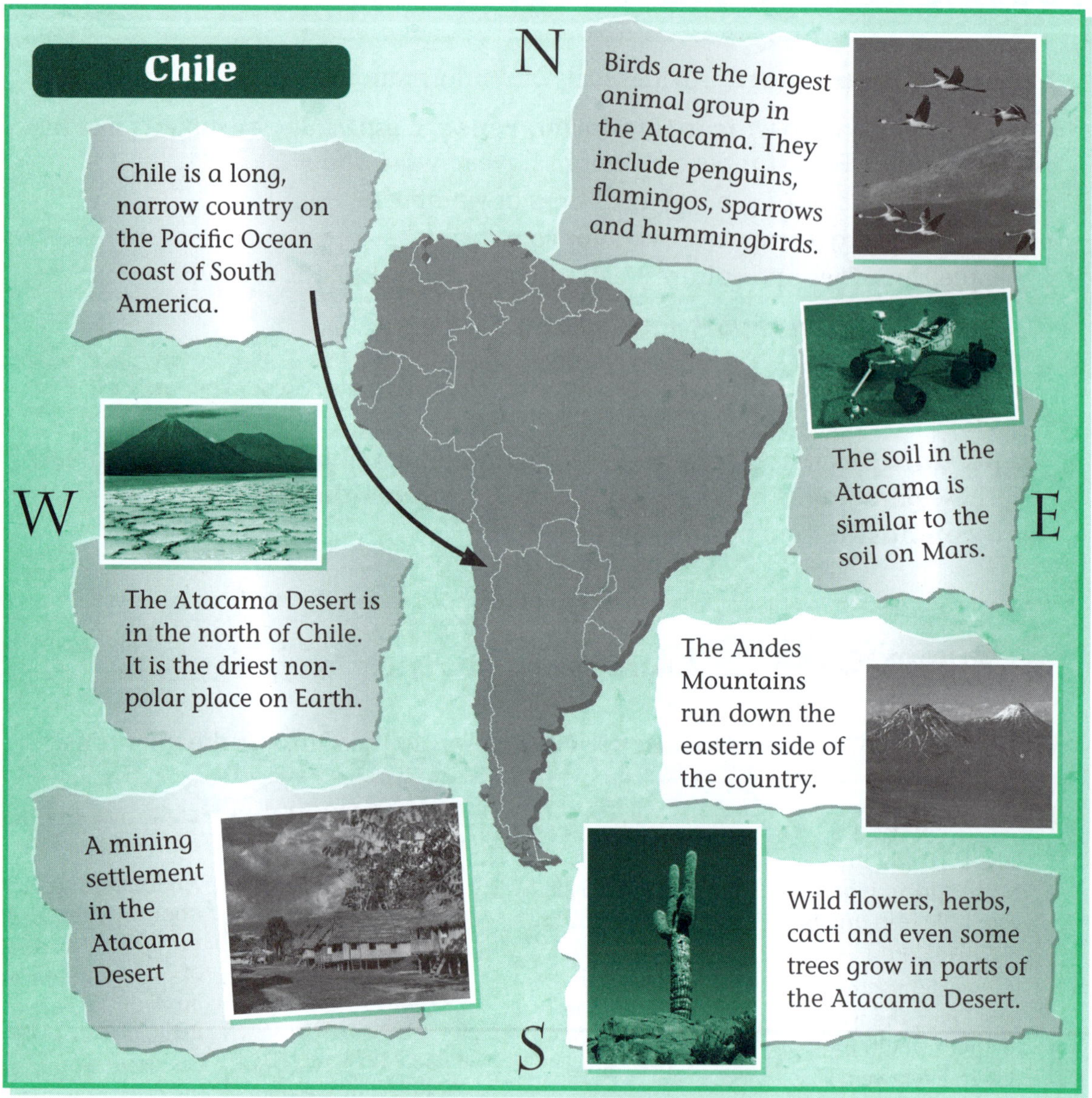

1. What do the following **abbreviations** stand for?

   a N ____________ **b** E ____________ **c** S ____________ **d** W ____________

2. Look at the map to work out the answers to the following. Circle the correct answer in each case.

   a Deserts occur on the (eastern, western, northern, southern) side of the continent.

   b The Pacific Ocean is on the (eastern, western, northern, southern) side of Chile.

3. Where in Chile would you expect to see penguins? ______________________

Writing the first draft

This is Logan's **first draft**. Read what he wrote and then answer the questions.

Hint! Logan has made some punctuation errors. See if you can spot them!

Chile

I have chosen Chile because I think it is an amazing country. It is long and narrow. It is on the west coast of South america.

Mountains

The andes mountain range is on the eastern side of the country. The part that runs through Chile has more than fifty active volcanoes. That sounds scary!

Weather

Chile is hot and dry in the north and gets cooler and wetter towards the south.

The Atacama Desert

The Atacama desert is in the northern part of the country. It is the driest non-polar place on earth.

Plants

Wild flowers, herbs, cacti and even some trees grow in parts of the atacama desert.

Animals

Not many animals live in the atacama desert. Some animals that live there are birds like penguins, flamingos, hummingbirds and sparrows. Insects, scorpions and reptiles like iguanas and lava lizards also live there.

People

Not many people live in the atacama. I definitely wouldn't want to live there! Most of the towns are on the coast. There are some mines further inland.

Conclusion

The soil in the Atacama desert is similar to the soil on mars.

1. A good **information report** should contain the following features. Tick (✓) the ones that Logan has used.

   a an **opening statement** or **introduction** that includes a **short description** of the subject ☐

   b **paragraphs** that give detailed information about the subject ☐

   c **subheadings** to organise the paragraphs ☐

   d only **facts**, not opinions ☐

   e **scientific language** (e.g. *temperature, Celsius*) ☐

   f **present-tense verbs** (e.g. *are, grow*) ☐

   g **capital letters** for the names of specific places ☐

   h a **conclusion** that rounds off the report ☐

2. Which adjectives has Logan used to describe:
   - **a** the volcanoes? ____________ ____________
   - **b** Chile's weather? ____________ ____________ ____________ ____________
3. Why do you think so few people and animals live in the Atacama Desert?

____

____

____

Step-by-step improvement plan

Logan is going to do some practice exercises to find ways to improve his draft. Help him complete them.

Step 1: Use capital letters for proper nouns

A **proper noun** is the name of a specific **person**, **place** or **thing**. All of the words in a proper noun start with a **capital letter**.
For example: *Sahara Desert, Nile River*

We use capital letters for proper nouns to show that they are **unique**.
For example: *The Nile River is different from all the other rivers in the world.*

Help Logan punctuate the following sentences correctly by rewriting the words that need **capital letters**.

1. Chile is on the western side of South america. ____________
2. The andes mountain range is on the eastern side of the country. ____________

   ____
3. The Atacama desert is in the northern part of the country. ____________
4. Part of the atacama desert is situated on the lower slopes of the andes.

   ____
5. NASA tests its instruments for future missions to mars in the Atacama because of its similarity to the red planet. ____________

Step 2: Use scientific language

Scientific language is language that is specific to a scientific subject.
For example: *climate, temperature* and *Celsius* (specific terms used to describe weather conditions)

Using **scientific language** in an information report shows that you have a good knowledge of your subject.

In these sentences, replace each underlined word or phrase with a more **scientific term** from the box.

flora and fauna	climate	an arid	experiences cooler temperatures
experiences temperatures of up to 25 degrees Celsius			

1. The Atacama Desert is a dry ______________ place that receives very little rainfall.
2. Chile is warm ______________________________ in the north.
3. Chile's weather ______________ changes as you move further south.
4. The southern part of Chile feels cooler ______________________________.
5. The Atacama is home to a variety of plants and animals. ______________________________.

Step 3: State facts, not opinions

A **fact** is something that can be proved to be true.
For example: *Deserts receive very little rainfall.*

An **opinion** is a personal view that may or may not be true.
For example: *Deserts are the worst places on Earth.*

An **information report** should contain **only facts**. It should **not** contain the writer's opinions.

1. Logan has expressed three **opinions** in his draft. Find them and underline them.
2. Circle the **facts** about flamingos, and put a line through the **opinions**.

Flamingos are birds.

Flamingos have long necks.

I think flamingos are great birds!

Flamingos are able to fly.

Flamingos are the most beautiful birds in South America.

Writing the final draft

This is Logan's **final draft**. Read the comments about his report on the left, and do the tasks on the right.

Comments

Tasks

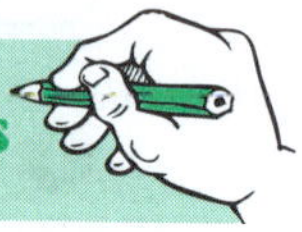

Chile

Start by giving a brief **definition** *of the subject.*

Chile is the longest country in the world. It measures more than 4500 km from north to south, but only about 150 km from west to east.

1. **Underline** the **adjective** that describes Chile's size.

Mountains

Using **subheadings** *tells your reader what the paragraph is about.*

The Andes Mountain Range is on the eastern side of the country. The part that runs through Chile has more than 50 active volcanoes.

2. **Highlight** the **proper nouns**.

Climate

In the north of Chile, the climate is hot and dry. The southern part has the coolest temperatures and the highest rainfall.

3. **Circle** the **scientific term** for *weather*.

The Atacama Desert

Using only **facts**, *not opinions, gives your reader reliable information.*

The Atacama Desert is an arid area in the northern part of the country. It is the driest non-polar place on Earth. Temperatures range between 0 and 25 degrees Celsius.

4. **Underline** the **proper nouns** that are the names of places.

Flora and fauna

Including **scientific language** *for the types of flora and fauna found in the region adds interest to your report.*

Wild flowers, herbs, cacti and even some trees grow in parts of the Atacama Desert. Birds are the largest animal group. They include penguins, flamingos, hummingbirds and sparrows. Other desert animals include insects, scorpions and a few reptiles, such as lava lizards and iguanas.

5. **Highlight** the **lists** of items.

People of the Atacama

Not many people live in the Atacama. Most of the towns are on the coast, although there are a few mining settlements further inland.

6. **Circle** the **phrase** that tells where most of the towns are.

Conclusion

The **conclusion** *rounds off the report in an interesting way.*

NASA (National Aeronautics and Space Administration) tests its instruments for future missions to Mars in the Atacama because of its similarity to the red planet.

7. **Underline** the **abbreviation** (shortened word or phrase).

Student B: Eleanor's draft

Eleanor, another Year 4 student, is going to write about Brazil.

She is using this poster to help her.

Look at the **information** on the poster.

1. Which **adjective** compares Brazil to all the other countries in South America?

   ____

2. Which **adjective** compares certain trees to all the other trees in the rainforest?

   ____

3. Which **adjective** describes:

   a the birds of the rainforest? ____________________

   b the mammals of the rainforest? ____________________

Writing the first draft

This is Eleanor's **first draft**. Read what she wrote and then answer the questions.

Brazil

Brazil is in South America.

Rivers

The amazon river is in Brazil. It is the largest river in the world. It is in the northern part of Brazil.

Weather

The equator and the tropic of capricorn are in Brazil. It is hot all the time around the equator. It rains a lot. It is cooler and drier in the south.

The Amazon rainforest

More than half of the Amazon rainforest is in Brazil. It is the biggest rainforest in the world.

Plants and animals

There are some very tall trees in the Amazon. They form a thick layer at the top of the forest. Underneath the plants are thinner. Only ferns, herbs and fungi grow at the bottom.

Lots of different animals live in the Amazon rainforest. Some of them are dangerous.

People of the Amazon

About 20 million people live in the Amazon. Most of them live in cities or towns. Some still live in the jungle.

Conclusion

The biggest threats to the future of the Amazon rainforest are the cutting down of trees and hotter weather.

1. Which of these features has Eleanor remembered to use in her draft? Tick (✓) the ones that Eleanor has used.

   - **a** an **opening statement** or **introduction** that includes a short **definition** or **description** of her subject ☐
   - **b** **paragraphs** that give **detailed information** about her subject ☐
   - **c** **subheadings** to organise her paragraphs ☐
   - **d** only **facts**, not opinions ☐
   - **e** **scientific language** (e.g. *Tropic of Capricorn*) ☐
   - **f** **present-tense verbs** ☐
   - **g** **capital letters** for all proper nouns ☐
   - **h** a **conclusion** that rounds off her report ☐

2 Answer the following questions in full sentences.

a Why do you think the plants underneath the top layer of trees are thinner?

____

____

b Why do you think the temperatures are cooler in the south of the country?

____

____

Step-by-step improvement plan

Eleanor is also going to do some practice exercises to find ways to improve her draft. Help her complete them.

Step 1: Start with a good opening statement

The **opening statement** is the first sentence or two of the report. It should contain a brief **description** of the subject to make the reader want to find out more.

Help Eleanor expand her **opening statement** by adding the following information.

Tip! You will need at least two sentences.

largest country in South America	eastern side of the continent	next to the Atlantic Ocean

Brazil is ____

____

____

____

Step 2: Use capital letters for proper nouns

Eleanor has also written some **proper nouns** with small letters. Use a red pen to fill in all the **capital letters** in the following sentences.

Reminder! All of the words in a proper noun start with a capital letter, except for small words like *and* or *of*.

1. Other important rivers in brazil include the parana and the negro.
2. More than half of the amazon rainforest is in brazil.

3. The equator and the tropic of capricorn run across brazil.
4. Countries that share a border with brazil include argentina, peru, bolivia and venezuela.
5. The gulf of mexico and the caribbean sea lie between south america and the united states of America.
6. The capital city of brazil is brasilia and the official language is portuguese.
7. Two of the largest cities in brazil are sao paulo and rio de janeiro.

Step 3: Use scientific language

Although Eleanor has used some **scientific language** in her draft, she could replace the underlined words and phrases below with more scientific terms. Help her choose the correct ones from the box.

the canopy, the understorey and the forest floor			
deforestation	a mainly tropical climate	indigenous	species
humid	climate change	flora and fauna	annual

1. The equator and the Tropic of Capricorn pass through Brazil, so the country has mainly hot and rainy weather. ______________________________ ______________________.
2. Around the equator it is hot and sticky ______________________ throughout the year.
3. The average yearly ______________________ temperature is about 27 degrees Celsius, and some places receive more than 2000 mm of rain per year.
4. One in ten of the world's known plant and animal types ______________ are found in the Amazon Rainforest.
5. The Amazon Rainforest is home to a wide variety of plants and animals ______________________________.
6. The rainforest can be divided into three sections: the top, the middle and the bottom ______________________________ ______________________.
7. There are still many native ______________________ people who rely totally on the river and the forest for their way of life.
8. The biggest threats to the future of the Amazon Rainforest are the cutting down of trees ______________________ and hotter weather ______________________.

Writing the final draft

Eleanor has started writing the **final draft** of her **information report**. Help her to complete it, and then look in the answers section to compare what you have written with what she wrote.

Hint! Look at the poster and the practice exercises for ideas.

Brazil

Brazil is the largest country in South America. It lies on the eastern side of the continent, next to the Atlantic Ocean.

Rivers

The world's largest river, the Amazon, runs through the northern part of the country. Other important rivers include the Parana and the Negro.

Climate (Describe Brazil's climate.)

....

....

....

....

The Amazon Rainforest

More than half of the Amazon Rainforest is in Brazil. It is the biggest rainforest in the world.

Flora and fauna

The rainforest consists of three sections: a thick canopy at the top of the forest, the understorey and the forest floor.

The forest is home to a wide variety of animals. (Describe the animals that are found in the rainforest.)

....

....

....

....

People of the Amazon

About 20 million people live in the Amazon. Most of them live in cities or towns, but there are still many indigenous people who rely totally on the river and the forest for their way of life.

Conclusion

(Describe the threats to the future of the rainforest.)

....

....

....

Your turn

Write an **information report** of about a page on one of the following. Use your own paper for this activity.

Writing Checklist Make sure your information report includes: ✓

- an **opening statement** that includes a **short description** of your subject. ☐
- a **detailed description** of the subject, presented as a **series** of **paragraphs**. ☐
- **paragraphs** with **headings** that tell the reader what each paragraph is about. ☐
- **facts**, not opinions. ☐
- **scientific language**. ☐
- **present-tense verbs**. ☐
- **correct spelling** and **punctuation**. ☐
- a **conclusion** that rounds off the report. ☐

Tip Use **Logan's final draft** on page 54 and **Eleanor's final draft** on page 59 to help you write your report.

Go to WORD BANK pages 105–106 for useful vocabulary

1. Write an information report about one of the following South American countries:

   a Peru. **b** Bolivia.

2. Use a map of Africa and the information below to help you write an information report about the Sahara Desert.

The Sahara is the world's largest hot desert.

The desert covers most of North Africa.

The desert is made up of sand dunes and hard, rocky ground. It is home to many species of rodents, snakes and scorpions.

The Sahara is bordered by the Atlantic Ocean in the west, the Red Sea to the east, the Mediterranean Sea to the north, and the grasslands of central Africa in the south.

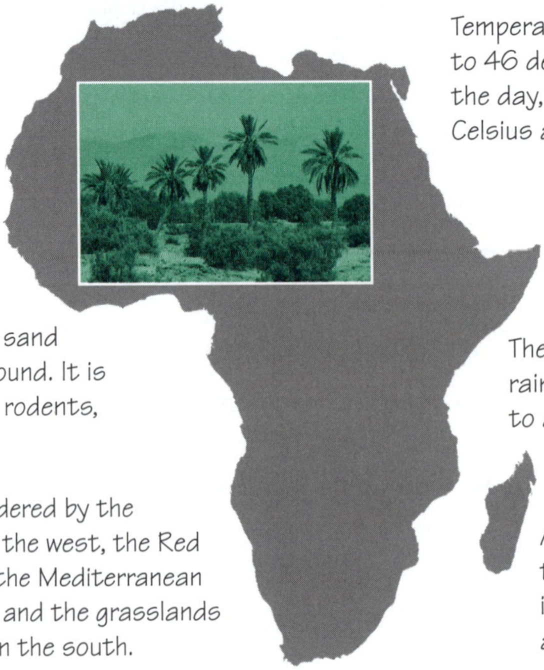

Temperatures range from 38 to 46 degrees Celsius during the day, to less than 0 degrees Celsius at night.

The main river in the Sahara is the Nile.

The Sahara receives very little rainfall—from less than 3 mm to about 100 mm annually.

An oasis is a place in the desert where water is found. People can live and grow crops there.

Unit 6 Writing a procedure

Looking at procedures

A **procedure** gives instructions on how to **make** or **do** something.

A leaflet that explains how to make a model and recipes are examples of procedures.

A **procedure** should have:

- an **introduction** that tells what you are going to make or do.
- a **list** of the ingredients or materials you will need.
- a **series of steps** or instructions, given in the correct order.

Hint! **Photographs**, **drawings** or **diagrams** are often included to help the reader understand the instructions.

Read the following **procedure** and then answer the questions.

Aboriginal hand stencils can be seen on rocks and cave walls throughout Australia.

This is how to make your own hand stencil.

What you need:
A sheet of black paper and some white paint powder.

Instructions:
First, wipe a damp cloth over the paper.

Next, place your hand in the centre of the paper.

Then, flick the paint powder over your hand and the paper.

Remove your hand, and there you have it—your own hand stencil!

1. Underline the sentence that tells what the purpose of the **procedure** is.
2. What **materials** are needed to make a hand stencil? ____________________
3. Circle the words that show the order in which the **steps** should be done.
4. Write down four action verbs in the instructions.

____

Student A: Naomi's draft

Naomi's Year 4 class are learning about the Aboriginal and Torres Strait Islander Peoples in history. Each student has to make something that relates in some way to the Indigenous people's way of life. They also have to write the **procedure** that explains how the item is made.

Naomi is going to make clap sticks, a type of musical instrument.

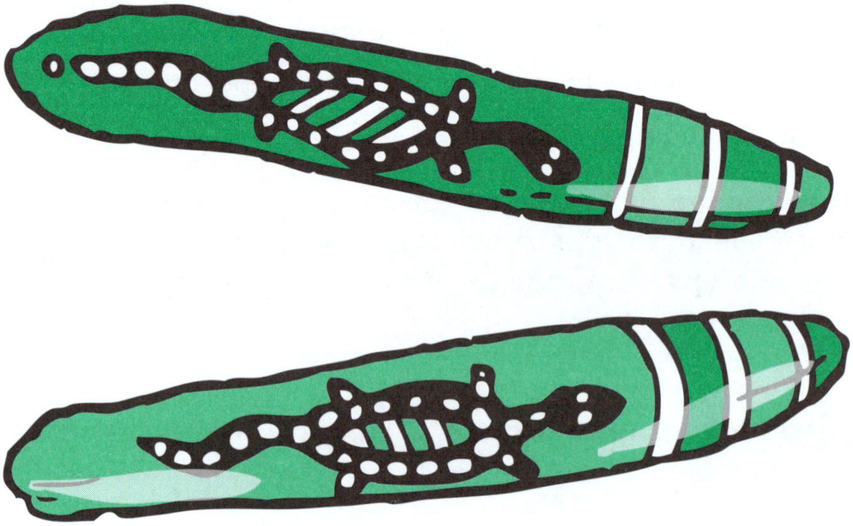

She starts by writing down a list of some of the materials she will need.

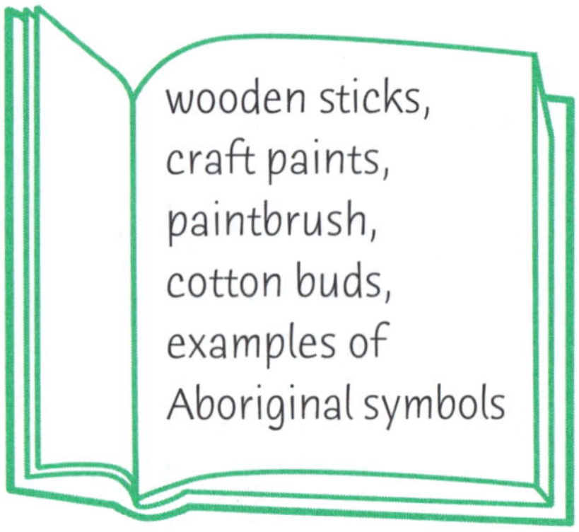

1. Why do you think Naomi needs examples of Aboriginal symbols?

2. What do you think Naomi is going to do with the cotton buds?

3. How do you think the clap sticks are used to make music?

Writing the first draft

This is Naomi's **first draft**. Read what she wrote and then answer the questions.

How to Make Clap Sticks

Clap sticks are traditional Aboriginal musical instruments. They are usually used with other instruments, such as the didgeridoo. They are clapped together to provide a beat for the music.

To make your own clap sticks, you will need the following materials:
sandpaper, two wooden dowel sticks, craft paints, palette, paintbrush, cotton buds, a toilet paper holder cut in half, examples of Aboriginal symbols

This is how you make the clap sticks:
Cover your work surface.
Use the sandpaper to make your dowel sticks smooth. Clean and dry them.
Cover the sticks with one of the colours. Let it dry.
Don't smudge the paint. Put them on the toilet roll holders.
Get more colours. Use the cotton buds to make patterns on the sticks.

1 A good **procedure** should contain the following features. Tick (✓) the ones that Naomi has used.

- **a** an **introduction** that tells what the **aim** or **purpose** of her procedure is ☐
- **b** a **list** of the **materials** that she will need ☐
- **c** a **series of steps**, or **instructions** ☐
- **d** sentences that start with **action verbs** (e.g. **Cover** *the work surface*) ☐
- **e** **connectives** that show the **order** in which the actions are done (e.g. *first, after that*) (Sometimes the steps are numbered instead.) ☐
- **f** **adverbs** that tell **how** the action should be done (e.g. *neatly, carefully*) ☐
- **g** **present-tense verbs** (e.g. *cover, use*) ☐
- **h** **correct spelling** and **punctuation** ☐

2 Naomi has given us some interesting information about clap sticks in her **introduction**.

a Which other Aboriginal musical instrument does she mention?

____

b What is the main purpose of clap sticks in Aboriginal music?

____

c If you'd never made clap sticks before, how hard would it be to make them using Naomi's draft?

easy ☐ very easy ☐ difficult ☐ very difficult ☐

Step-by-step improvement plan

Naomi is going to do some practice exercises to find ways to improve her draft. Help her complete them.

Step 1: Add interest with descriptive verbs

A **verb** is a word that shows that an **action** is happening.
For example: **Cover** *your work surface.*

Some verbs are more **descriptive** than others.
For example: **Flick** *the paint powder over your hand.*

Flick is more descriptive than, for example, *put*, because it tells you exactly how to apply the paint powder.

Using descriptive verbs makes your instructions easier to understand.

Replace each underlined **verb** with a more descriptive one from the box.

wipe	dip	spread	rub	squeeze

1. Smooth ________________ your dowel sticks with sandpaper.
2. Clean ________________ the dowel sticks with a damp cloth.
3. Put ________________ the paint onto your palette.
4. Put ________________ the paint over your dowel sticks.
5. Put ________________ a cotton bud into your first colour.

Step 2: Use adverbs to describe how something is done

Adverbs give **information about verbs**. They can make instructions clearer by telling exactly **how** something should be done.
For example: *quickly, slowly*

1. Complete each sentence with an **adverb** from the box.

frequently	clearly	carefully	securely	evenly

a Tie the pieces together ____________________.

b ____________________ pour the paint into the container.

c Brush the paint ____________________ over your dowel sticks.

d Check on the mixture ____________________.

e Write your name ____________________ on the label.

2 Find an **adverb** in the box to complete each sentence. Make sure you choose one that starts with the correct letter.

thoroughly	neatly	damply	respectfully	directly
nearly	exactly	extremely	regularly	tightly

a Change the water r________________.

b Paste the pictures n________________ onto the page.

c Hold the stick t________________ while you apply the paint.

d Draw lines that are e________________ 3 cm apart.

e Apply the paint d________________ onto the wood.

Step 3: Use connectives to show order

Connectives show the **order** in which actions are done.
For example: *First, next, then*

They help the reader make sense of your instructions.

1 Fill in the gaps in these instructions with **connectives** from the box. Make sure the connectives match the order in which the actions are done.

Then	Finally	First	Next

__________, cover your work surface with a plastic cloth.

__________, rub your dowel sticks lightly with sandpaper.

Wipe them with a damp cloth and leave them to dry.

__________, paint your dowel sticks.

Carefully place the sticks on the toilet roll holders and leave them to dry.

__________, decorate your sticks with dots and lines.

2 Use the **connectives** in the box to complete this short procedure.

After that	Meanwhile	First of all

________________, mix acrylic paint with water in small bowls. Make sure you use different colours.

________________, pour the paint into ice cube trays. Insert a paddle pop stick in the middle of each cube and place the tray in the freezer.

________________, cover a table with a plastic cloth and remove a sheet of paper from your sketchpad.

When the paint mixture has frozen, remove the cubes from the tray and spread the different coloured paints randomly over your paper.

Writing the final draft

This is Naomi's **final draft**. Read the comments about her **procedure** on the left, and do the tasks on the right.

Comments

Providing background information about the item in the ***introduction*** *adds interest to the procedure.*

Giving a ***list*** *of the materials needed helps the reader get organised.*

Using ***headings*** *and* ***paragraphs*** *makes the procedure easier to understand.*

Using ***connectives*** *shows the order in which the actions should be done.*

Using ***adverbs*** *tells the reader how the actions should be done.*

How to Make Clap Sticks

Clap sticks are traditional Aboriginal musical instruments. They are usually used with other instruments, such as the didgeridoo. They are clapped together to provide a beat for the music.

To make your own clap sticks, you will need the following materials:

two wooden dowels (about 15–20 cm long and the width of a broomstick), sandpaper, craft paints, a palette, a paintbrush, cotton buds, a toilet paper holder cut in half, examples of Aboriginal symbols

This is how you make the clap sticks:

First, cover your work surface with a plastic cloth.

Then, rub your dowel sticks lightly with sandpaper.

Wipe them with a damp cloth and leave them to dry.

Next, squeeze your background colour onto your palette.

Spread the paint evenly over your dowel sticks.

Carefully place the sticks on the toilet roll holders and leave them to dry.

Squeeze the colours you're going to use for your designs onto the palette.

Dip a cotton bud into your first colour, making sure you don't cover the bud too thickly.

Apply the paint as a series of dots.

Repeat with the other colours until your design is complete.

Tasks

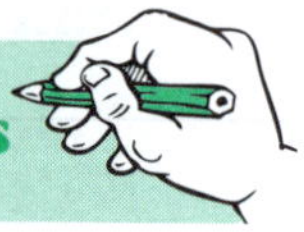

1. **Circle** three **adjectives** that describe the noun *instruments*.
2. **Underline** the extra information about the wooden dowels.
3. **Highlight** the **connective**.
4. Circle the **adverb**.
5. **Highlight** the **action verb**.
6. **Underline** two **adverbs**.
7. **Circle** the **contraction** (shortened word).
8. **Highlight** the **adverb**.
9. **Highlight** the **phrase** that tells how to apply the paint.

Student B: Damian's draft

Damian, another Year 4 student, is going to make this tablemat based on the types of mats Aboriginal and Torres Strait Islanders used to weave. He is going to use pictures of Aboriginal artwork to help him make the mat.

Images woven to make mat

Damian also starts by writing a list of the materials and equipment he will need.

two sheets of A4 paper, a ruler, a pencil, scissors, sticky tape and A4 laminating pouch

access to a computer, printer and laminating machine

1. Why do you think Damian needs access to a computer and printer?

2. Why would it be a good idea for Damian to laminate his tablemat?

Writing the first draft

This is Damian's **first draft**. Read it and then answer the questions.

How to Weave a Tablemat

Aboriginal and Torres Strait Islander people used natural materials like bark and feathers to weave items such as baskets, mats, bags and nets.
This is how you can make your own woven tablemat using modern materials.

Materials

two sheets of A4 paper, a ruler, a pencil, scissors, sticky tape, an A4 laminating pouch
access to a computer, printer and laminating machine

Steps

Get two pictures of Aboriginal art on the internet.
Print them out.
Cut away the white parts around the edges and turn one of the pictures over.
Make a border around the edge and draw lines 2 cm apart down the page.
Fold the page in half lengthwise and cut along the lines.
Cut the other page into lengthwise strips 2.5 cm wide.
Put the strips through the first page and stick everything down at the back.
Laminate your mat.

1 Which of these things has Damian remembered to include in his draft? Tick (✓) the correct answers.

- **a** an **opening statement** that tells his reader what the **aim** of the procedure is ☐
- **b** a **list** of the **materials** he will need ☐
- **c** a **series of steps** or instructions ☐
- **d** **sentences** that **start** with **action verbs** ☐
- **e** **connectives** or numbers to show the **order** in which the **actions** should be done ☐
- **f** **adverbs** that tell **how** the **action** should be done ☐
- **g** **present-tense verbs** ☐
- **h** **correct spelling** and **punctuation** ☐

2 How easy would it be to make this mat using Damian's draft?

easy ☐ | very easy ☐ | difficult ☐ | very difficult ☐

Step-by-step improvement plan

Damian is also going to do some practice exercises to find ways to improve his draft. Help him complete them.

Step 1: Add interest with descriptive verbs

Choose the more **descriptive verb** in brackets to complete each sentence.

1. (Get, Find) ____________________ pictures of Aboriginal artwork on the internet.
2. (Trim, Cut) ____________________ away the white paper around each image.
3. (Make, Draw) ____________________ a border around the edge of the paper.
4. (Put, Weave) ____________________ the strips of paper through the slits in the first image.
5. (Neaten, Fix) ____________________ your mat by taping down the strips of paper at the back.
6. (Cover, Protect) ____________________ your mat by laminating it.

Step 2: Use adverbs to describe how something is done

1. Complete each sentence with an **adverb** from the box. Use each adverb once. Be careful though—some of the adverbs can be used in more than one sentence.

exactly	approximately	accurately	carefully

   a ____________________ measure a 1-cm border around one of the images.

   b Draw lines ____________________ 2 cm apart parallel to the short sides.

   c ____________________ weave the strips of paper through the slits in the other image.

   d Draw lines ____________________ 2.5 cm apart parallel to the long sides of the second image.

2. Complete each sentence with the **adverb** that is similar in meaning to the underlined words and phrases.

immediately	gradually	completely	almost	diagonally

   a Add the water bit by bit ____________________ to the mixture.

   b Draw a line at an angle ____________________ across the page.

   c Remove it from the container straight away ____________________.

   d Place the canvas on the table when the paint is nearly ____________________ dry.

   e Apply the paint so that it covers the surface all over ____________________.

Step 3: Use connectives to show order

The following instructions follow one after the other. Make this clear by filling in suitable **connectives** from the box.

afterwards	after that	before	finally	first
first of all	in the meantime	meanwhile	next	then

______________________, trim away the white paper around each image.

Turn the images to the blank side and accurately measure a 1-cm border around one of them.

______________________, draw lines exactly 2 cm apart parallel to the short sides. Make sure the lines are inside the border.

______________________, carefully fold the image in half lengthwise so that the edges all meet.

Cut along the parallel lines up to the borders you drew earlier.

______________________, draw lines approximately 2.5 cm apart parallel to the long sides of the second image.

Use the lines to help you cut the second image into even strips.

______________________, weave the strips through the slits in the first image, creating an interesting pattern.

Examples of Aboriginal artwork

Writing the final draft

Damian has started writing the **final draft** of his **procedure**. Help him complete it, and then look in the answers section to compare what you have written with what Damian wrote.

Hint! Look at Damian's notes and the practice exercises for ideas.

How to Weave a Small Mat

Aboriginal and Torres Strait Islander people used natural materials like bark and feathers to weave items such as baskets, mats, bags and nets.

This is how you can make your own woven tablemat using modern materials.

Materials

two sheets of A4 paper, a ruler, a pencil, scissors, sticky tape, an A4 laminating pouch
access to a computer, printer and laminating machine

Steps

Start by finding two pictures of Aboriginal art on the internet. Download and print them out.

(Complete the sentences where necessary.)

Trim away the white paper around each image.

Turn the images to the blank side and accurately measure a 1-cm border around one of them.

Draw in the border with a pencil and ruler.

Next, draw ....

....

Make sure the lines are inside the border.

After that, carefully fold ....

....

Cut along the parallel lines up to the borders you drew earlier.

Then, draw lines approximately 2.5 cm apart parallel to the long sides of the second image.

Use the lines to help you cut the second image into even strips.

Finally, weave ....

....

Use sticky tape to secure the strips at the back of your mat.

Place your woven mat into a laminating pouch, making sure the borders around the edges are even.

Once you've laminated your mat, it's ready to use at the dinner table!

Your turn

Write a **procedure** of about one page on one of the following. Use your own paper for this activity.

Writing Checklist Make sure your procedure includes: ✓

- an **opening statement** that tells what the **aim** or **purpose** of the procedure is. ☐
- a **list** of the **ingredients**, **utensils**, **equipment** or **materials** that will be needed. ☐
- a clear **set of steps**, or instructions, given in the **correct order**. ☐
- **sentences** that **start** with **action verbs**. ☐
- **connectives** or numbers to show the **order** in which the **actions** should be done. ☐
- **adverbs** that tell **how** the **actions** should be done. ☐
- **present-tense verbs**. ☐
- **correct spelling** and **punctuation**. ☐

Tip Use **Naomi's final draft** on page 66 and **Damian's final draft** on page 71 to help you write your procedure.

Go to **WORD BANK** page 106 for useful vocabulary

1. Look on the internet or in a book for information on how to make something that is part of Aboriginal culture, e.g. a boomerang or a didgeridoo. Write the procedure that explains how to make the item, using simple materials such as cardboard or foam board. Use Naomi and Damian's procedures as models.
2. Use simple materials such as cardboard and paint to make the Australian flag, and then write the procedure that tells others how to make it. Use the photograph to help you.
3. Write instructions for a craft activity that you really like doing.

Unit 7 Writing a narrative

Looking at narratives

A **narrative** tells a story based on a real or imagined event. Its main **purpose** is to **entertain**, but some narratives give us interesting information about people and events. Stories about the past, for example, can show us what life was like for our ancestors.

A **narrative** should have:

- an **orientation**, or **beginning**, that sets the scene, usually by telling **who**, **what**, **where** and **when**.
- a **build-up** to a **complication** or **problem** that has to be **solved**.
- a **series of events** that result from the **complication**.
- an **ending** or **resolution**, in which the problem is **solved**.

Read this student's version of the fairytale *Goldilocks and the Three Bears,* and then answer the questions.

One day Goldilocks was walking in the woods when she saw a little house.

She was tired and hungry. She knocked on the door. There was no one at home, so she went inside. On the table were three bowls of steaming porridge—a big one, a medium-sized one and a small one. Goldilocks sat down to eat from the biggest bowl, but the chair was too hard and the porridge too hot. Then she tried some of the porridge from the medium-sized bowl. This time the chair was too soft and the porridge too salty. Finally she sat on the smallest chair and ate from the smallest bowl. The porridge was delicious, but she was too heavy for the chair and it broke!

Then she went upstairs. She saw three beds, a big one, a medium-sized one and a small one. She lay down on the small one. It was perfect, and immediately she fell fast asleep.

When the bears came home, they saw that someone had been eating their porridge. Baby Bear took one look at his broken chair and empty bowl and started to howl!

Goldilocks woke with a start. She apologised for eating Baby Bear's porridge. She said she'd been starving.

Mother Bear told her not to worry. She made some more porridge for Baby Bear, and she even offered some to Goldilocks.

1. Look at the orientation. Where does the story take place? ____________________
2. The complication in the story is when the bears come home and find Goldilocks in their house. Explain how the problem is solved.

____

____

Student A: Musa's draft

Musa's Year 4 class have to write a **narrative** based on a proverb.

First, their teacher wrote some proverbs on the board and the class discussed what they meant.

1 Every cloud has a silver lining. (Something good can come out of a bad situation.)

2 Don't count your chickens before they're hatched. (Don't rely on something before it happens.)

3 Practice make perfect. (The more you practise something, the better you get at it.)

4 The early bird catches the worm. (The one who gets there first has the best chance of success.)

5 You can't judge a book by its cover. (You can't tell what someone or something is like just by looking at them.)

Musa remembered how he had misjudged one of the boys in his class at the beginning of the year. He decided to base his narrative on that experience.

The first thing he did was plan his narrative.

Orientation: Who? Mr Stiles, Joshua, Adam, Chen, Hyun
What? Joshua—new boy
Where? in classroom
When? beginning of term

Build up: Mr Stiles chooses Hyun to be Joshua's buddy—Hyun not one of the cool kids—Joshua looks like a cool kid

Complication: Cool crowd angry—want Joshua to be part of their group

Event 1: Hyun dreading recess—thinks Adam and Chen will make fun of him in front of Joshua

Event 2: Recess—Adam and Chen want Joshua to play cricket with them at lunch break

Resolution: Joshua says he'd rather play chess with Hyun—Hyun very happy—says he misjudged Joshua

1 Use words and phrases from Musa's plan to complete the following sentence.

Hyun didn't think Joshua would be his buddy because ______________________________

____

2 Explain how the proverb *You can't judge a book by its cover* was true in Joshua's case.

____

____

____

Writing the first draft

This is Musa's **first draft**. Read what he wrote, and then answer the questions.

You Can't Judge a Book by Its Cover

Mr Stiles introduced the new boy to the class. His name was Joshua. He was tall, with a friendly face. Adam and Chen smiled at him. He smiled back. I could see they wanted him to join the cool crowd.

I knew Mr Stiles wouldn't make me his buddy. I wasn't one of the cool kids. Then Mr Stiles said I must be Joshua's buddy. I was surprised.

Joshua sat next to me. He smiled at me and said hello. The boys in the cool crowd weren't happy.

Then it was time for recess. I was worried. Adam and Chen would try to get Joshua to join their crowd. They would make fun of me in front of Joshua.

When they asked Joshua if he wanted to play cricket with them at lunch break, he said no, he wanted to play chess with me. Mr Stiles told him I was a brilliant player.

I felt so happy. I remembered the proverb we'd learnt in class about not judging a book by its cover. I had misjudged Joshua.

1. A good **narrative** should contain the following features. Tick (✓) the ones that Musa has used.
   - **a** a clear **orientation** that sets the scene by telling **who**, **what**, **where** and **when** ☐
   - **b** a **problem** that has to be **solved** ☐
   - **c** a **series of events**, divided into **paragraphs** ☐
   - **d** **descriptive verbs** (e.g. *whispered, dashed*) ☐
   - **e** **past-tense verbs** (e.g. *was, sat*) ☐
   - **f** interesting **information** and **detail** about the events ☐
   - **g** **correct spelling** and **punctuation** ☐
   - **h** a strong **resolution** that shows how the problem is solved and wraps up the story ☐

2. Musa has used some good **adjectives** to add interest to his narrative.
   - **a** Which two adjectives describe Joshua's appearance? ______________________

     ____
   - **b** Which adjective describes how Hyun felt when it was time for recess?

     ____
   - **c** Which adjective describes what kind of chess player Hyun was?

     ____

Step-by-step improvement plan

Musa is going to do some exercises to find ways to improve his **narrative**. Help him complete them.

Step 1: Start with an interesting orientation

The **orientation** is the first paragraph or two of the narrative. It needs to be **interesting** to hook the reader in.

Which of these **orientations** is more likely to grab the reader's attention and make them want to read further?

1. "This is Joshua," said Mr Stiles. The boy standing next to him was tall, with a friendly face. ☐

2. The new boy standing next to Mr Stiles was tall and had a friendly face. Mr Stiles said his name was Joshua. ☐

Step 2: Add interest with descriptive verbs

Verbs can tell us what **action** is happening and **when** it happens.
For example: *He* ***introduced*** *the new boy.*

Some verbs are more descriptive than others; for example, *whispered* is more descriptive than *said* because it tells us exactly **how** the person spoke.

Using descriptive verbs in a **narrative** makes the story more interesting to read.

Choose the more **descriptive verb** in brackets to complete each sentence.

1. I (saw, noticed) ________________ Adam and Chen smile at him.
2. He greeted me, and I (mumbled, said) ________________ something back.
3. Adam and Chen were (scowling, looking) ________________ at us.
4. Adam and Chen (walked, swaggered) ________________ up to us.
5. We (strolled, walked) ________________ slowly across the playground.

Step 3: Add colour with figurative language

Figurative language is language that doesn't mean exactly what it says; for example, *Max has a heart of gold* doesn't mean Max's heart was made of gold; it means he was kind and generous.

Using figurative language in a narrative makes it more **interesting** to read.

Match the sentence on the left with the emotion it expresses on the right.

Figurative language	Literal meaning
1 I was walking on air.	**a** approval
2 I had butterflies in my stomach.	**b** surprise
3 They gave him the thumbs up.	**c** nervousness
4 He couldn't believe his ears.	**d** happiness
5 They were looking daggers at me.	**e** anger

Step 4: Bring the characters to life with dialogue

Dialogue is the actual words someone says in a text. It can help bring your characters to life.

It is important that you punctuate dialogue correctly.

- Use **speech marks** (" ") around the actual words that a character says, **including** any punctuation.
- Use a **capital letter** when someone speaks for the first time, even if the first spoken word comes after a comma.
- Start a **new paragraph** when a new character starts speaking.

For example: "What's your name?" asked Mr Stiles.

"It's Joshua," replied the new boy.

Hint! Don't ruin your narrative with too much dialogue.

Fill in the missing speech marks in the following sentences.

1. Hyun, said Mr Stiles, I want you to be Joshua's buddy this term.
2. Why me? Hyun whispered to the boy sitting next to him.
3. Joshua smiled at me. Hello, he said in a confident voice.
4. Hello, I mumbled back, not looking at him.
5. Mr Stiles says you're a good cricketer, Josh, said Adam. How'd you like to play with us at lunch break? Hyun doesn't know anything about cricket.
6. No thanks, said Joshua, I'd rather play chess with Hyun.
7. Mr Stiles says he's a brilliant player, said Joshua.
8. Well, said Hyun, you can't always judge a book by its cover.

Writing the final draft

This is Musa's **final draft**. Read the comments about his **narrative** on the left, and do the tasks on the right.

Comments

A good **orientation** *gets the reader's attention.*

An interesting **complication** *draws the reader in.*

Using **dialogue** *helps bring the characters to life.*

Using **figurative language** *adds colour to the narrative.*

Using **descriptive verbs** *makes the story more interesting to read.*

The **resolution** *solves the problem and wraps up the story.*

You Can't Judge a Book by Its Cover

"This is Joshua," said Mr Stiles. The boy standing next to him was tall, with a friendly face. I noticed Adam and Chen give each other the thumbs up. That meant they were going to invite him to join the cool crowd. They smiled at him and he smiled back.

Mr Stiles always gave new students a buddy with the same interests as them. I was sure he wouldn't choose me. I wasn't one of the cool kids.

"Hyun, I want you to be Joshua's buddy this term," said Mr Stiles. Me? I couldn't believe my ears! Everyone in the class looked in my direction. Adam and Chen were scowling.

Joshua walked over to my desk and sat down beside me. He smiled. "Hello," he said.

"Hello," I mumbled.

All morning I could feel the boys in the cool crowd looking daggers at me, but Joshua didn't seem to notice.

Finally the bell rang for recess. I had butterflies in my stomach. I knew that Adam and Chen were going to make fun of me in front of Joshua, and that Joshua would decide that he'd rather be buddies with them.

Sure enough, as soon as we got outside, Adam and Chen swaggered up to us.

"Mr Stiles says you're a good cricketer, Josh," said Adam. "How'd you like to play with us at lunch break? Hyun doesn't know anything about cricket."

"No thanks," said Joshua. "I'd rather play chess with Hyun, if he doesn't mind. Mr Stiles says he's a brilliant player."

I was walking on air as Joshua and I strolled across the playground. I remembered the proverb we'd learnt in class about not judging a book by its cover. I had definitely misjudged Joshua.

Tasks

1. **Highlight** the **adjectives** that describe Joshua.
2. **Circle** the **word** that means the same as *select*.
3. **Underline** an example of **figurative language**.
4. **Highlight** the **actual** words the boys said.
5. **Underline** the example of **figurative language**.
6. **Highlight** the **sentence** that shows Hyun was nervous.
7. **Circle** the **descriptive verb**.
8. **Underline** the **sentence** that asks a question.
9. **Circle** the **adjective**.
10. **Highlight** the **expression** that shows that Hyun was very happy.

Student B: Adina's draft

Adina, another Year 4 student, remembered the time she nearly had to give up piano lessons because she wasn't practising enough. She based her narrative on the proverb *Practice makes perfect.*

She also started by planning her **narrative**.

Orientation: Who? Lisa, Mrs Naidu
What? Lisa has a music lesson
—hasn't practised
When? That afternoon
Where? Mrs Naidu's house

Build-up: Lisa plays for Mrs Naidu—Mrs Naidu disappointed in her

Complication: Mrs Naidu says Lisa will have to stop her music lessons

Event 1: Lisa begs for another chance

Event 2: Practises hard all week

Resolution: Goes to music lesson—plays well—Mrs N says it was perfect—Lisa says practice made it perfect.

Use Adina's notes to help you answer the following questions.

1 Why do you think Mrs Naidu told Lisa she'd have to stop her music lessons?

____

____

____

2 When Mrs Naidu told Lisa she'd have to stop her music lessons, Lisa most likely felt:

- **a** happy. ☐
- **b** excited. ☐
- **c** upset. ☐
- **d** angry. ☐

3 Explain how the proverb *Practice makes perfect* was true in Lisa's case.

____

____

____

Writing the first draft

This is Adina's **first draft**. Read what she wrote and then answer the questions.

Practice Makes Perfect

It was time for Lisa's music lesson. She didn't want to go. She hadn't practised enough.

Her teacher, Mrs Naidu, was waiting for her. Lisa loved Mrs Naidu, and she loved playing the piano. She didn't want to disappoint Mrs Naidu. She wished she'd practised more.

When Mrs Naidu asked Lisa if she'd been practising, Lisa said she had. She was cross with herself for lying.

She played the first piece. She looked at Mrs Naidu. She could see how disappointed her teacher was in her. Mrs Naidu said if she didn't start practising, she would have to give up music lessons. Lisa asked for another chance. She said she would practise harder.

The following week she practised lots and lots. She was excited when she went to her next music lesson.

She played the first piece. Mrs Naidu was smiling. She said it was perfect.

Yes, thought Lisa, *it was practice that made it perfect.*

1 Which of these features has Adina remembered to include in her draft? Tick (✓) the ones that Adina has used.

- **a** a clear **orientation** that tells **who**, **what**, **when** and **where** ☐
- **b** a **problem** that has to be **solved** ☐
- **c** a **series of events** divided into **paragraphs** ☐
- **d** **descriptive verbs** ☐
- **e** **past-tense verbs** ☐
- **f** interesting **information** and **detail** about the events ☐
- **g** **correct spelling** and **punctuation** ☐
- **h** an interesting **resolution** that shows how the problem is **solved** ☐

2 Use the information in Adina's draft to complete the following sentences.

a Lisa didn't want to go to her music lesson because ______________________

____

b Lisa didn't want to give up music lessons, so ______________________

____

Step-by-step improvement plan

Adina is also going to do some practice exercises to find ways to improve her draft. Help her complete them.

Step 1: Start with an interesting orientation

Adina has written another **orientation** for her narrative.

> Lisa wasn't looking forward to her music lesson. It was that afternoon. She wished she'd spent less time watching TV. She wished she'd spent more time practising.

Help Lisa improve her new **orientation** by turning the following pairs of sentences into a single sentence.

Hint! You need to leave out some words in the second sentence in each case. You will also need to use the **conjunction** *and* in one of the sentences.

1. Lisa wasn't looking forward to her music lesson. It was that afternoon.

   ____

   ____

2. She wished she'd spent less time watching TV. She wished she'd spent more time practising. ______________________________

   ____

Step 2: Add interest with descriptive verbs

1. Help Lisa make her narrative more interesting by replacing the underlined **verbs** with more descriptive ones from the box.

glanced	exclaimed	beaming	murmured	begged

a When Mrs Naidu asked Lisa if she'd been practising, Lisa <u>said</u> ________________ that she had.

b When she'd finished playing, Lisa <u>looked</u> ________________ at her teacher.

c Lisa <u>asked</u> ________________ Mrs Naidu to give her another chance.

d Mrs Naidu was <u>smiling</u> ________________.

e Mrs Naidu <u>said</u> ________________ that it was perfect.

2 In the following lists, highlight the words that are another way of saying:

a looked.
- peeped
- peered
- crept
- scanned
- stared
- dozed
- glimpsed

b asked.
- beseeched
- prodded
- pleaded
- revealed
- implored
- requested
- demanded

c run.
- dart
- shove
- flutter
- rush
- race
- drip
- dash

Step 3: Add colour with similes and metaphors

Similes compare one thing to something else using the words *like* or *as*.
For example: *Lisa was **as** nervous **as** a kitten.*
*Lisa was **like** a nervous kitten.*

Metaphors compare one thing to something else by saying that it is that thing.
For example: *Lisa was a bundle of nerves.*

Similes and **metaphors** help the reader create mind pictures of people, places and events. Like descriptive verbs, they add interest to the text.

Are the following sentences **similes** or **metaphors**? Write the answers in the spaces.

1 Lisa practised so much her fingers felt like jelly. ______________________

2 Lisa felt a tingle of excitement run up her spine. ______________________

3 Mrs Naidu was grinning as broadly as a Cheshire cat. ______________________

Step 4: Bring the characters to life with dialogue

Use a red pen to fill in the missing **capital letters** and **speech marks** in the following sentences.

1 good morning, Lisa, said Mrs Naidu brightly. How did you get on with the two pieces I set you last week?

not too badly, murmured Lisa, looking down at her feet.

2 Lisa, said Mrs Naidu, if you don't start practising, we'll have to stop your music lessons.

3 that was perfect, Lisa! she exclaimed.

Writing the final draft

Adina has started writing the **final draft** of her **narrative**. Help her complete it by filling in the missing sections, and then look in the answers section to compare what you have written with what Adina wrote.

Hint! Look at Adina's first draft and practice exercises for ideas.

Practice Makes Perfect

Lisa wasn't looking forward to her music lesson that afternoon. She wished she'd spent less time watching TV and more time practising.

Lisa loved Mrs Naidu, her teacher, and wanted to please her. She also loved playing the piano. But every week it was the same story—she didn't practise enough. She wasted her time watching silly programs on TV or playing computer games.

When Lisa got to Mrs Naidu's house, her teacher was waiting for her.

(How did Mrs Naidu greet Lisa, and what was Lisa's reply to Mrs Naidu's question?)

....

....

....

....

Lisa sat down at the piano and started playing. At the end of the first piece, she glanced at her teacher. She could see the disappointment on Mrs Naidu's face. But worse was to come.

"Lisa," said Mrs Naidu, "if you don't start practising, we'll have to stop your music lessons."

(What did Lisa beg Mrs Naidu to do?)

....

....

The following week, Lisa practised every day. She played the piano so much her fingers sometimes felt like jelly. But she knew she would be well prepared for her next lesson.

As she sat down to play the first piece, a tingle of excitement ran up her spine. When she had finished, she looked at Mrs Naidu. Her teacher was beaming from ear to ear.

(What did Mrs Naidu say to Lisa, and what was the thought that went through Lisa's mind?)

....

....

....

....

....

Your turn

Write a **narrative** of about a page on one of the following. Use your own paper for this activity.

Writing Checklist Make sure your narrative includes: ✓

- a **title**. ☐
- an **orientation** that captures the reader's attention and sets the scene by telling **who**, **what**, **where** and **when**. ☐
- an interesting **complication** or problem that has to be solved. ☐
- a **series of events** divided into **paragraphs**. ☐
- **interesting adjectives** and **descriptive verbs**. ☐
- interesting **information** and **detail** about the events. ☐
- a **resolution** in which the problem is **solved**. ☐

Tip Use **Musa's final draft** on page 78 and **Adina's final draft** on page 83 to help you write your narrative.

Go to WORD BANK page 106 for useful vocabulary

Write a **narrative** based on one of the following proverbs.

1. Every cloud has a silver lining.

   (Something good can come out of a bad situation.)

2. Don't count your chickens before they're hatched.

   (Don't rely on something before it happens.)

Unit 8 Writing a discussion

Looking at discussions

A **discussion** is a text in which you give the points **for** and **against** an idea and come up with a **conclusion**.

You and your parents might, for example, have talked about pocket money and come up with arguments for and against the idea.

A written discussion is similar, but you also have to come up with a conclusion about the idea.

Let's think about the question: *Should children get pocket money*? Here are some arguments for and against and one possible conclusion.

Arguments for:	Pocket money teaches children responsibility. It teaches them the value of money.
Arguments against:	Children could spend the money on the wrong things. They could lose the money if they carry it around with them.
Conclusion:	Children should get pocket money.

A **discussion** should have:

- an **introduction** that states the idea.
- **arguments for** the idea.
- **arguments against** the idea.
- a **conclusion** that tells whether you agree or disagree with the idea. Sometimes it can give advice.
  For example: *I think children should get pocket money, as long as they don't spend it on the wrong things.*

Read the **discussion** about homework and then do the activities.

1. Highlight the argument **for** homework.
2. Underline the argument **against** homework.
3. Put a box around the writer's **advice**.

Should Children Get Homework?

Many children do not like to do homework. There are lots of arguments for giving homework, but there are also arguments against it.

On the one hand, homework helps students practise things they learn in class.

On the other hand, children need to relax after school, not do more schoolwork.

I think homework is a good thing, but teachers mustn't give too much.

Student A: Ruby's draft

Ruby's Year 4 class are reading *Charlie and the Chocolate Factory* by Roald Dahl. In the novel, any child who finds a golden ticket in their chocolate bar will receive a lifetime supply of chocolates and sweets.

Each of the students has to write a **discussion** in which he or she looks at arguments for and against children eating chocolates and lollies.

Their teacher put some of their arguments on the board.

Should Children Eat Lollies and Chocolates?

Arguments for and against

lots of sugar

a delicious treat

good for parties

can make us sick

tooth decay

could spoil our appetite for healthier foods

make us happy

make good presents

Help Ruby organise the arguments by writing them in the correct columns.

For	Against
a ______	**a** ______
b ______	**b** ______
c ______	**c** ______
d ______	**d** ______

Writing the first draft

This is Ruby's **first draft**. Read what she wrote and then answer the questions.

> **Should Children Eat Chocolates and Lollies?**
>
> Most children like chocolates and lollies.
>
> Chocolates and lollies make them happy. This is a good thing. Adults give children lollies to cheer them up. Chocolates and lollies make good presents. Birthday parties wouldn't be as much fun without lollies.
>
> Chocolates and lollies are full of sugar. Sugar isn't healthy. It can cause tooth decay. Lollies can spoil children's appetites. They won't eat healthy food. They could get sick.

1. A good **discussion** should contain the following features. Tick (✓) the ones that Ruby has used in her draft.

   a an **introduction** that refers to the question and also states that there are **arguments** for and against the idea ☐

   b **arguments for** the idea ☐

   c **arguments against** the idea ☐

   d **connectives** to link ideas (e.g. *On the one hand* or *also*) ☐

   e **present-tense verbs** (e.g. *is* or *give*) ☐

   f **correct punctuation** and **spelling** ☐

   g a **conclusion** that tells whether you agree or disagree with the idea and that may also give **advice** ☐

2. Singular nouns show that there is only one person or thing. What is the singular of:

   a lollies? ________________ **b** parties? ________________

3. What is the word *won't* short for?

   would not ☐ will not ☐ will never ☐

4. Why has Ruby used an **apostrophe** (') in the word *children's*?

   ____

   ____

Step-by-step improvement plan

Ruby is going to do some exercises to find ways to improve her **discussion**. Help her complete them.

Step 1: Start with a good introduction

The **introduction** is the first paragraph. It should tell your reader what the discussion question is. It should also tell your reader that there are arguments for and against the idea. It should not say what your opinion is.

1 Which is the best way for Ruby to start her **discussion**? Tick (✓) the correct answer.

A All children love chocolates and lollies. I think they should be allowed to eat them. ☐

B Some children like chocolates and lollies but others don't. If they like them, they should be allowed to eat them. ☐

C Some people think children shouldn't eat chocolates and lollies. There are arguments for and against this idea. ☐

2 This is another way that Ruby could start her **discussion**. Fill in the missing parts.

Most children like ______________________________. Some people think they should be allowed ______________________________, but others ____________________. There are ______________________________ for and ____________________ on ____________________ sides.

Step 2: Link ideas with connectives

Connectives are words and phrases that link ideas in a text (e.g. *In addition* or *Furthermore*). They help make our writing flow.

Complete the following sentences with **connectives** from the box. Use each connective once.

Hint! Start with *On the one hand.*

However	On the other hand	therefore	On the one hand

1 ______________________________, eating chocolates and lollies makes children happy.

2 ______________________________, chocolates and lollies are full of sugar.

3. Chocolates and lollies are delicious. ______________________, they can cause tooth decay.
4. Eating lollies could spoil your appetite; __________________ you may not want to eat healthier foods like fruit and vegetables.

Step 3: End with a good conclusion

The **conclusion** is the last paragraph. This is where you give your overall opinion after thinking about both sides of the question. You can also give advice in this paragraph.

Choose from the list below the best **advice** Ruby could give to complete this sentence.

I think it is all right for children to eat chocolates and lollies, ______________

____

____

____

____

____

a as long as they are all the same colour.

b but they mustn't eat too many because they aren't good for you.

c especially if they really like them.

Writing the final draft

This is Ruby's **final draft**. Read the comments about her **discussion** on the left, and do the tasks on the right.

Comments

Tasks

Should Children Eat Chocolates and Lollies?

The ***introduction*** *should refer to the question and state that there are arguments for and against it.*

Most children love chocolates and lollies. Some people think they should be allowed to eat them but others don't. There are arguments for and against on both sides.

1. **Underline** the word that has a similar meaning to *like*.

Giving ***arguments for*** *and* ***against*** *the idea helps the reader make a decision.*

Using ***connectives*** *to link ideas makes the writing flow.*

On the one hand, eating chocolates and lollies makes children happy. This is a good thing. Adults often give children lollies to cheer them up when they are sad or upset. Chocolates and lollies also make good presents because most children like to eat them. In addition, birthday parties wouldn't be as much fun if children didn't have lollies to eat.

2. **Highlight** the sentences that start with a **connective**.

On the other hand, chocolates and lollies are full of sugar. Sugar is not a healthy food. It can cause tooth decay. Eating too many lollies can also spoil children's appetites. They might not eat as much fruit and vegetables as they should. If they don't eat healthy food, they could get sick.

3. **Underline** the **connective** at the beginning of the paragraph.

The ***conclusion*** *gives the writer's overall opinion after thinking about both sides of the question. It can also give advice.*

I think it is all right for children to eat chocolates and lollies, but they mustn't eat too many.

4. **Highlight** the writer's **advice**.

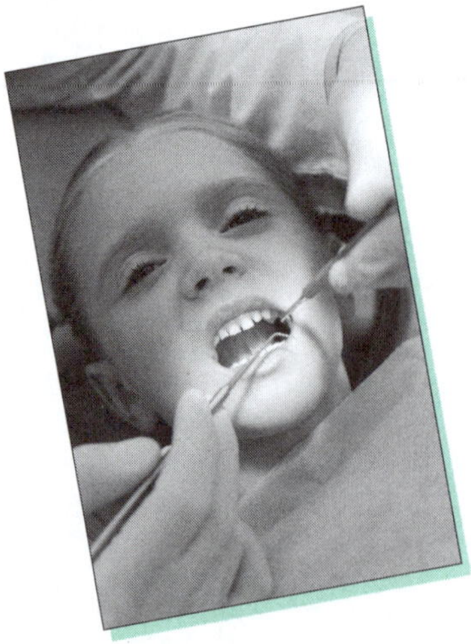

Student B: Aran's draft

One of the characters in *Charlie and the Chocolate Factory* is Mike Teavee. He spends all his time watching television.

The Year 4 students have to write another **discussion** in which they look at arguments for and against children watching television.

One of the students, Aran, wrote these arguments in his notebook.

Should Children Be Allowed to Watch Television?

Arguments for and against

television programs can be entertaining

some programs contain violence

can learn a lot from some programs

don't get any exercise watching television

children enjoy watching television

watching television could be bad for children's health

some programs are educational

many programs not suitable for children

Help Aran organise his **arguments** by writing them in the correct columns.

For	Against
a	a
b	b
c	c
d	d

Writing the first draft

This is Aran's **first draft**. Read it and then answer the questions.

Should Children Be Allowed to Watch Television?

There are arguments for and against letting children watch television.

On the one hand, many television programs are entertaining. Children enjoy watching them. This makes them happy. Television programs are also educational. Children learn a lot from them. They can watch documentaries like *Frozen Planet*. They can even learn how to cook. They can watch the food programs.

On the other hand, many television programs are not suitable for children. They contain violence. This is not a good thing. Also, children may not get enough exercise. They sit and watch television all the time. This is bad for their health.

Overall, I think that watching television is good for children.

1 Which of these features has Aran remembered to use in his draft? Tick (✓) the correct answers.

- **a** an **introduction** that refers to the **question** and also states that there are **arguments** for and against the idea ☐
- **b** **arguments for** the idea ☐
- **c** **arguments against** the idea ☐
- **d** **connectives** to link ideas ☐
- **e** **present-tense verbs** ☐
- **f** a **conclusion** that tells whether the writer agrees or disagrees with the idea and also gives advice ☐

2 Aran has remembered to link some of his ideas with connectives.

Underline three **connectives** that Aran has used in his draft.

3 In the draft, find the **nouns** that are formed from the words below. Write the nouns in the spaces.

argue	violent	healthy
____________	____________	____________

4 Write down the **plural** of *documentary*. ____________

Step-by-step improvement plan

Aran is also going to do some exercises to find ways to improve his **discussion**. Help him complete them.

Step 1: Start with a good introduction

1. Which is a good way for Aran to start his **introduction**? Tick (✓) the correct answer.

A These days most people have a television in their homes. But should children be allowed to watch it? ☐

B I think children should be allowed to watch television. Most children like to watch it. ☐

2. This is another way Aran could write his **introduction**. Fill in the missing sections.

Most children like watching ____________________. But is it a good thing for children to do? There are arguments __________________________________

______________________________.

Step 2: Join clauses with conjunctions

A **clause** is a group of words that contains a verb.
For example: *I* **am watching** *television. The program* **is** *educational.*

Conjunctions join clauses, and words within clauses.
For example: *Ruby* **and** *Aran can watch television* **because** *they have finished their homework.*

Joining clauses with conjunctions makes our writing flow.

Join the following words and clauses with a **conjunction** from the box. Use each conjunction once.

if	and	because	or	but

1. Children enjoy watching television ________________ it makes them happy.
2. Some television programs are educational ________________ children learn a lot from them.
3. Children might even learn how to cook ________________ they watch the food programs.
4. Many television programs are suitable for children ________________ some contain violence.
5. Children should not watch programs that contain violence ________________ bad language.

Step 3: Ending with a good conclusion

1. Read Aran's **conclusion** again:

   Overall, I think that watching television is good for children.

   What has he left out? Tick (✓) the correct answer.

   a a statement in which he agrees or disagrees with the idea ☐

   b advice for the readers ☐

2. Help Aran write a better **conclusion** for his discussion by filling in the missing words and phrases from the box.

too much	bad language	allowed	violence

   Overall, I think that children should be ____________________ to watch television, as long as they don't watch ____________________. They also shouldn't watch programs that contain ____________________ and ____________________.

3. What other advice could Aran give his readers about the programs children shouldn't watch?

   Use the **phrase** on the note to help you write your sentence.

   programs that are rated PG or M

   ____

   ____

   ____

   ____

   ____

   ____

Writing the final draft

Aran has started writing the **final draft** of his **discussion**. Help him complete it by filling in the missing sections, and then look in the answers section to compare what you have written with what Aran wrote.

Hint! Look at Aran's notes and the practice exercises for ideas.

Write a good introduction for Aran's discussion.

On the one hand, children enjoy watching television because many programs are entertaining. They make children happy. Lots of programs are also educational, like *Frozen Planet*. Children can learn a lot from them. If children watch the food programs, they can even learn how to cook.

On the other hand, **(Continue the paragraph, giving arguments against children watching television.)**

Overall, I think that children should be allowed to watch television, but they shouldn't watch too much. Also, they shouldn't be allowed to watch programs that have lots of violence and bad language in them.

Your turn

Write a **discussion** of about a page on one of the following. Use your own paper for this activity.

Writing Checklist Make sure your discussion includes: ✓

- an **introduction** that refers to the **question** and states that there are **arguments** for and against the idea ☐
- **arguments for** and **against** the idea ☐
- **connectives** to **link ideas** ☐
- **conjunctions** to **join** words and clauses ☐
- **present-tense verbs** ☐
- a **conclusion** that tells whether you agree or disagree with the idea and gives **advice** ☐

Tip Use **Ruby's final draft** on page 90 and **Aran's final draft** on page 95 to help you write your discussion.

Go to WORD BANK page 106 for useful vocabulary

1. Should children get paid for doing chores around the house?
2. Should sport be a school subject?
3. Use the pictures below to help you write arguments for and against building a pool in the backyard.

Answers

Unit 1 Writing a recount

Page 1

1 hundreds of aunts, uncles and cousins
2 in the UK
3 to spend Christmas and New Year with relatives
4 it's freezing here and it rains a lot

Page 2

1 a Yum! b Yay! c It was fun!
d boring e again! f more fun!
2 a play computer games and watch TV.
b we won our soccer match./my friend George came to my house./I got to play with my cousins.

Page 3

1 a, b, c, e, f 2 did, spent, came, played, ate

Pages 4–5

Step 1

2 In the afternoon/After lunch
3 That night/Later 4 The next morning
5 After lunch/In the afternoon
6 Later/That night

Step 2

1 two boring 2 a brilliant
3 my funny green 4 a very good
5 traditional Lebanese 6 a young

Step 3

1 b
2 I had a busy weekend, but it was great fun!

Page 6

1 went 2 strawberry 3 After lunch, then
4 That night 5 were
6 traditional Lebanese food, an old family tradition
7 When dinner was over
8 I really enjoyed spending time with my family and friends over the weekend.

Page 7

1 a exciting! b brilliant!
2 a new b final c lucky d great
3 a celebrating b celebrations
c celebrates d celebrated

Page 8

1 b, c, d, e, f 2 had, washed, gave, got, saw
3 a outfit b parade c performers

Pages 9–10

Step 1

A

Step 2

1 On Saturday morning 2 After that/Then
3 Then/After that 4 In the evening/That night
5 The next day 6 After lunch
7 That night/In the evening 8 Finally

Step 3

1 a outfit b celebrations c lunch
d restaurant e floats f display
2 a talented b colourful/spectacular
c spectacular/colourful

Step 4

The New Year celebrations ended with a spectacular fireworks display, and then it was time to go home. I thought this year's celebrations were the best ever, but Mum says I say that every year!

Pages 11–12

My weekend

The weekend was one of the busiest and most exciting times of the year for me. It was Chinese New Year!

On Saturday morning I went shopping with Mum. We had to buy clothes and lots of other exciting things for the New Year celebrations.

After that, I helped Mum clean the house. Then I washed my hair and tried on my new outfit. It looked amazing! Later I helped Mum put up the final decorations.

The next day we went to my favourite restaurant in the city where we met other members of our family and some special friends. My grandparents, aunts, uncles and cousins were there. It was so exciting! It's a tradition in our culture for the grownups to give children lucky money at New Year. They put the money in red envelopes because the Chinese consider red to be a lucky colour. I got lots of red envelopes and I'm feeling very rich!

After lunch we watched the New Year parade. We saw talented acrobats, dancers, martial artists and other performers in the parade. I really liked the floats. They were so colourful. I also liked the dragon and lion dances.

The New Year celebrations ended with a spectacular fireworks display, and then it was time to go home. I thought this year's celebrations were the best I'd ever seen, but Mum says I say that every year!

Unit 2 Writing a description of an animal

Page 13

1 b 2 b

Page 14

1 thick, rough, big, heavy, white, black
2 They can't run very fast.
3 It means their risk of becoming extinct is very high.

Page 15

1 a, b, c, d, f, g 2 eats, run, climb
3 It has small ears.

Pages 16–17

Step 1

1 massive 2 stumpy 3 cute
4 cuddly 5 coarse 6 enormous

Step 2

1 and 2 but 3 and
4 so 5 and 6 Although

Step 3

1 Its eyes, ears, legs and shoulders are black.
2 It is covered in thick, coarse fur.
3 If you ever see one of these animals, it will most likely be in a zoo.
4 These animals will sleep anywhere, but they like to lean back against something.
5 These animals have powerful teeth and jaws to help them chew the leaves, stems and shoots of bamboo plants.
6 Because the nutritional level of bamboo is low, these animals use as little energy as possible.

Page 18

1 big, enormous 2 will help
3 head, thick, coarse eyes, ears, legs black,
4 and but 5 leaves, stems low, my
6 cute, cuddly

Page 19

1 They are set close together.
2 They are set quite far above the mouth.
3 It's an omnivore.

Page 20

1 a, b, c, d, f, g
2 a long, reddish-brown b long, curved
3 to help it climb trees

Pages 21–22

Step 1

1 bulky 2 powerful 3 (an) enormous
4 fresh 5 bowed

Step 2

1 which 2 who 3 whose 4 that 5 who

Step 3

1 and 2 Although 3 but
4 because 5 When

Step 4

1 long, reddish-brown
2 fruits, leaves, stems, insects
3 long arms, fingers 4 to sleep, it makes
5 are curved, so it is

Page 23

My Favourite Animal

My favourite animal lives in forests. It is intelligent and is about seven times stronger than a human.

My animal has a bulky body and is quite big. It is covered in long, reddish-brown hair.

My animal, which has long, powerful arms, is good at climbing trees. When it stretches out its arms, its arm span measures about 2 metres from fingertip to fingertip. When it stands, its hands almost touch the ground.

My animal has four fingers and a thumb on each hand and five toes on each foot. Its fingers and toes are long and curved to help it grip onto branches when it climbs trees. It does not have a tail.

Although my animal has short, bowed legs, it can stand and walk upright. It can also walk on all fours.

My animal sleeps in trees. Before it goes to sleep at night, it makes a fresh nest.

It eats food that it finds in the forest, like fruit, leaves, stems, bark, insects and honey.

Those of you who have seen my animal in a zoo should easily guess what it is.

Unit 3 Writing a sound poem

Page 25

1 a moon b place c yet d croak
2 c

Page 26

1 whistling, purring, ticking 2 crunching
3 the frying pan
4 a away b clock c makes d fill

Page 27

1 a 2 **Suggestions**: glug-glug, gulp
3 joke, coke 4 No

Pages 28–29

Step 1

1 Talking words: whispering, muttering
Shouting words: shrieking, squealing
Crying words: sobbing, whining
Laughing words: chuckling, giggling
Singing words: chanting, humming
Gasping words: panting, puffing
Snoring words: snorting, snuffling
Moaning words: grumbling, groaning

2 Suggested answers:
a stuttering, stammering, chattering, jabbering
b bellowing, yelling, whooping, screeching

3 burping, sniffing, yawning, hiccupping, munching, clapping

Step 2

1 dear, fear, near, here, cheer, appear
2 long, wrong, along, thong, strong
3 sell, well, swell, smell, tell, yell, shell

Page 30

1 ear, fear 2 chuckling, slurping
3 song, wrong 4 cheering, squeals

Page 31

1 the drain 2 swishing 3 crying, squeaking
4 drumming 5 bawling, wailing

Page 32

1 a, b
2 a barking, meowing, crying, oink, sing, quack, hoot
b geese, frogs, hens, cows, sheep, bees, lion, mouse

Pages 33–34

Step 1

1 geese—cackling, lion—roaring, frogs—croaking, mouse—squeaking, hens—clucking, cows—mooing, birds—twittering, sheep—baaing, seagulls—squawking, bees—buzzing

2 Dogs: growling, howling, snarling, woofing
Birds: cheeping, tweeting, chirping, cooing
Bees: humming, droning, murmuring

3 a hissing b chattering c whining

Step 2

1 dogs: frogs, logs, jogs, fogs
cats: bats, mats, plaits, rats, gnats
seagull: dull, hull, skull
hens: pens, wrens, tens, dens
cows: meows, bows, rows
bees: sneeze, knees, trees
ducks: sucks, clucks, trucks
mouse: house, grouse, louse

2 a ringing b sounds c rams

3 songs: clangs, sons, sings
ewes: two, sweets
lowing: browning, flowering

Page 35

The Sounds Animals Make

The cackling of the geese
The barking of the dogs
The meowing of the cats
The croaking of the frogs
The squawking of the seagulls
The clucking of the hens
The mooing of the cows
Grunting pigs inside their pens
The baaing of the sheep
The buzzing of the bees
The roaring of the lions
Birds cheeping in the trees
The quacking of the ducks
The squeaking of a mouse
The hooting of an owl
As it flies above our house

Unit 4 Writing to persuade—expositions

Page 37

1 a 2 b

Page 38

1 keeps hair out of your face; helps keep you cool on a hot day
2 stops you losing papers or posters; makes it easier to carry things
3 can wear it on your wrist; helps you remember to get forms signed

Page 39

1 a, b, c, d, e, h, i 2 think, believe 3 definitely
4 **Suggestions**: You can roll it into a ball and use it as an eraser.
You can wrap it around your pencil to give you a better grip.

Pages 40–41

Step 1

Number 1

Step 2

Firstly, In addition, also, Secondly, for example, Finally

Step 3

1 if/when 2 when/if 3 because

4 so 5 but/although

Step 4

Number 3

Page 42

1 I definitely think the rubber band is the most useful item to have in your school bag.

2 If, when, or, so 3 Secondly, For example

4 slipping a rubber band around your wrist

5 but

Page 43

1 repairs things

2 holds things together

3 can bend it into different shapes

Page 44

1 a, b, c, e, h, i

2 **Suggestions**: You can use it as a hairclip. You can use it as a bookmark.

3 **Suggestions**: I think the paperclip is more useful because rubber bands often snap if you stretch them too far.

Pages 45–46

Step 1

Number 2

Step 2

1 If 2 until 3 and 4 or 5 so

Step 3

Firstly, For example, also, Secondly, In addition, Finally, for instance

Step 4

Suggestion: I've only given you a few examples of the different ways you can use a paperclip. However, I'm sure my arguments have convinced you that it is the most useful of the six items.

Page 47

Why the Paperclip Is the Most Useful Item

I would definitely choose the paperclip to have in my school bag. Actually, I would have quite a few of them. I think the paperclip is by far the most useful of the six items, for the following reasons.

Firstly, a paperclip is handy for fixing things. For example, if the pages of your book come loose, a paperclip will keep them in place until you can get them fixed. A paperclip can also be turned into a little pin that can be used for all sorts of things, like unclogging the little opening at the top of a glue bottle.

Secondly, paperclips are good for holding things together. They help you keep your notes or papers organised, and they are perfect for sealing plastic bags. In addition, you can use paperclips to attach photos, cards or anything else to a piece of string to make a classroom display.

Finally, you can bend a paperclip into different shapes, so you can be very creative with it; for instance, you can turn it into a hook or sculpture.

I've only given you a few examples of the different ways you can use a paperclip. However, I'm sure my arguments have convinced you that it is the most useful of the six items.

Unit 5 Writing an information report

Page 49

1 a, d 2 in the Nile River 3 c

Page 50

1 a North b East c South d West

2 a western b western

3 along the coast

Pages 51–52

1 a, b, c, f, h

2 a fifty, active b hot, dry, cooler, wetter

3 **Suggestion**: So few people and animals live in the Atacama Desert because there's hardly any water there and both people and animals need water to survive.

Pages 52–53

Step 1

1 America 2 Andes Mountain Range

3 Desert 4 Atacama Desert, Andes 5 Mars

Step 2

1 an arid

2 experiences temperatures of up to 25 degrees Celsius

3 climate 4 experiences cooler temperatures

5 flora and fauna

Step 3

1 I have chosen Chile because I think it is an amazing country.

That sounds scary!

I definitely wouldn't want to live there!

2 **Facts**: Flamingos are birds.

Flamingos have long necks.

Flamingos are able to fly.

Page 54

1 longest 2 Andes Mountain Range, Chile

3 climate 4 Atacama Desert, Earth

5 wild flowers, herbs, cacti and even some trees
penguins, flamingos, hummingbirds and sparrows
insects, scorpions and a few reptiles

6 on the coast 7 NASA

Page 55

1 largest 2 tallest

3 a colourful b unusual

Pages 56–57

1 b, c, d, e, f, g, h

2 a The plants underneath the top layer of trees are thinner because they don't receive as much sunlight.

b The temperatures become cooler the further you move away from the equator.

Pages 57–58

Step 1

Suggestion: Brazil is the largest country in South America. It is on the eastern side of the continent, next to the Atlantic Ocean.

Step 2

1 Brazil, Parana, Negro

2 Amazon Rainforest, Brazil

3 Tropic of Capricorn, Brazil

4 Brazil, Argentina, Peru, Bolivia, Venezuela

5 Gulf of Mexico, Caribbean Sea, South America, United States of America

6 Brazil, Brasilia, Portuguese

7 Brazil, Sao Paulo, Rio de Janeiro

Step 3

1 a mainly tropical climate 2 humid

3 annual 4 species 5 flora and fauna

6 the canopy, the understorey and the forest floor

7 indigenous 8 deforestation, climate change

Page 59

Brazil

Brazil is the largest country in South America. It lies on the eastern side of the continent, next to the Atlantic Ocean.

Rivers

The world's largest river, the Amazon, runs through the northern part of the country. Other important rivers include the Parana and the Negro.

Climate

The equator and the Tropic of Capricorn pass through Brazil, so the country has a mainly tropical climate. Around the equator it is hot and humid throughout the year. The average annual temperature is about 27 degrees Celsius, and some places receive more than 2000 mm of rain per year. The climate is cooler and drier in the south.

The Amazon Rainforest

More than half of the Amazon Rainforest is in Brazil. It is the biggest rainforest in the world.

Flora and fauna

The rainforest consists of three sections: the canopy, the understorey and the forest floor.

The forest is home to a wide variety of animals. These include colourful birds, like toucans and macaws, and mammals like sloths and tamarin monkeys. There are also lots of dangerous animals in the forest, such as jaguars, anacondas, piranha fish and poison dart frogs.

People of the Amazon

About 20 million people live in the Amazon. Most of them live in cities or towns, but there are still many indigenous people who rely totally on the river and the forest for their way of life.

Conclusion

The biggest threats to the future of the Amazon Rainforest are deforestation (the cutting down of trees) and climate change.

Unit 6 Writing a procedure

Page 61

1 This is how to make your own hand stencil.

2 a sheet of black paper and some white paint powder

3 First, Next, Then 4 wipe, place, flick, Remove

Page 62

1 She needs to see what the symbols look like so that she can decorate her clap sticks.

2 She is going to use them to dot paint onto the clap sticks.

3 They are clapped together.

Page 63

1 a, b, c, d, g, h

2 a didgeridoo

b Clap sticks provide a beat for the music.

c Answers will vary.

Pages 64–65

Step 1

1 Rub 2 Wipe 3 Squeeze

4 Spread 5 Dip

Step 2

1 a securely b Carefully c evenly
d frequently e clearly

2 a regularly b neatly c tightly
d exactly e directly

Step 3

1 First, Then/Next, Next/Then, Finally
2 First of all, After that, Meanwhile

Page 66

1 traditional Aboriginal musical
2 (about 15–20 cm long and the width of a broomstick)
3 First 4 lightly 5 squeeze
6 evenly, Carefully 7 you're
8 thickly 9 as a series of dots

Page 67

1 He needs the computer to find images of Aboriginal artwork and a printer to print them out.
2 If Damian laminates his tablemat, it will protect it and make it last longer.

Page 68

1 **a, b, c, d, g, h** 2 Answers will vary.

Pages 69–70

Step 1

1 Find 2 Trim 3 Draw
4 Weave 5 Neaten 6 Protect

Step 2

1 a Accurately b exactly/approximately
c Carefully d approximately/exactly
2 a gradually b diagonally
c immediately d almost
e completely

Step 3

First/First of all, trim away the white paper around each image.

Turn the images to the blank side and accurately measure a 1-cm border around one of them.

Afterwards/After that/Next/Then, draw lines exactly 2 cm apart parallel to the short sides. Make sure the lines are inside the border.

Afterwards/After that/Next/Then, carefully fold the image in half lengthwise so that the edges all meet.

Cut along the parallel lines up to the borders you drew earlier.

Afterwards/After that/Next/Then, draw lines approximately 2.5 cm apart parallel to the long sides of the second image.

Use the lines to help you cut the second image into even strips.

Finally, weave the strips through the slits in the first image, creating an interesting pattern.

Page 71

How to Weave a Tablemat

Aboriginal and Torres Strait Islander people used natural materials like bark and feathers to weave items such as baskets, mats, bags and nets.

This is how you can make your own woven tablemat using modern materials.

Materials

two sheets of A4 paper, a ruler, a pencil, scissors, sticky tape, an A4 laminating pouch

access to a computer, printer and laminating machine

Steps

Start by finding a picture of Aboriginal art on the internet. Download and print it in colour and as a black-and-white image.

Trim away the white paper around each image.

Turn the images to the blank side and accurately measure a 1-cm border around one of them.

Draw in the border with a pencil and ruler.

Next, draw **lines exactly 2 cm apart parallel to the short sides.** Make sure the lines are inside the border.

After that, carefully fold **the image in half lengthwise so that the edges all meet.**

Cut along the parallel lines up to the borders you drew earlier.

Then, draw lines approximately 2.5 cm apart parallel to the long sides of the second image.

Use the lines to help you cut the second image into even strips.

Finally, weave **the strips through the slits in the first image, creating an interesting pattern.**

Use sticky tape to secure the strips at the back of your mat.

Place your woven mat into a laminating pouch, making sure the borders around the edges are even.

Once you've laminated your mat, it's ready to use at the dinner table!

Unit 7 Writing a narrative

Page 73

1 in the woods
2 Mother Bear forgave Goldilocks and made more porridge.

Page 74

1 Hyun didn't think Joshua would be his buddy because he wasn't one of the cool kids.
2 Hyun thought Joshua would want to be friends with the cool crowd, but Joshua liked chess and wanted to be friends with Hyun.

Page 75

1 a, b, c, e, f, g, h

2 a tall, friendly b worried c brilliant

Pages 76–77

Step 1

Number 1

Step 2

1 noticed 2 mumbled 3 scowling
4 swaggered 5 strolled

Step 3

1—d; 2—c; 3—a; 4—b; 5—e

Step 4

1 "Hyun," said Mr Stiles, "I want you to be Joshua's buddy this term."
2 "Why me?" Hyun whispered to the boy sitting next to him.
3 Joshua smiled at me. "Hello," he said in a confident voice.
4 "Hello," I mumbled back, not looking at him.
5 "Mr Stiles says you're a good cricketer, Josh," said Adam. "How'd you like to play with us at lunch break? Hyun doesn't know anything about cricket."
6 "No thanks," said Joshua, "I'd rather play chess with Hyun."
7 "Mr Stiles says he's a brilliant player," said Joshua.
8 "Well," said Hyun, "you can't always judge a book by its cover."

Page 78

1 tall, friendly 2 choose
3 I couldn't believe my ears. 4 Hello Hello
5 looking daggers at me
6 I had butterflies in my stomach. 7 swaggered
8 How'd you like to play with us at lunch break?
9 brilliant 10 I was walking on air

Page 79

1 Lisa wasn't practising enough, so Mrs Naidu probably thought Lisa was wasting her time learning to play the piano.
2 c
3 Lisa played the piano perfectly after she had practised a lot.

Page 80

1 a, b, c, e, f, g, h
2 a Lisa didn't want to go to her music lesson because she hadn't practised enough.
b Lisa didn't want to give up music lessons, so she decided to practise harder.

Pages 81–82

Step 1

1 Lisa wasn't looking forward to her music lesson that afternoon.
2 She wished she'd spent less time watching TV and more time practising.

Step 2

1 a murmured b glanced c begged
d beaming e exclaimed
2 a peeped, peered, scanned, stared, glimpsed
b beseeched, pleaded, implored, requested, demanded
c dart, rush, race, dash

Step 3

1 simile 2 metaphor 3 simile

Step 4

1 "**G**ood morning, Lisa," said Mrs Naidu brightly. "How did you get on with the two pieces I set you last week?"
"**N**ot too badly," murmured Lisa, looking down at her feet.
2 "Lisa," said Mrs Naidu, "if you don't start practising, we'll have to stop your music lessons."
3 "**T**hat was perfect, Lisa!" she exclaimed.

Page 83

Practice Makes Perfect

Lisa wasn't looking forward to her music lesson that afternoon. She wished she'd spent less time watching TV and more time practising.

Lisa loved Mrs Naidu, her teacher, and wanted to please her. She also loved playing the piano. But every week it was the same story—she didn't practise enough. She wasted her time watching silly programs on TV or playing computer games.

When Lisa got to Mrs Naidu's house, her teacher was waiting for her.

"Good morning, Lisa," said Mrs Naidu brightly. "How did you get on with the two pieces I set you last week?"

"Not too badly," murmured Lisa, looking down at her feet. *Liar*, she thought.

Lisa sat down at the piano and started playing. At the end of the first piece, she glanced at her teacher. She could see the disappointment on Mrs Naidu's face. But worse was to come.

"Lisa," said Mrs Naidu, "if you don't start practising, we'll have to stop your music lessons."

Lisa begged Mrs Naidu to give her another chance.

The following week, Lisa practised every day. She played the piano so much her fingers sometimes felt like jelly. But she knew she would be well prepared for her next lesson.

As she sat down to play the first piece, a tingle of excitement darted up her spine. When she had finished, she looked at Mrs Naidu. Her teacher was beaming from ear to ear.

"That was perfect, Lisa!" she exclaimed.

Yes, thought Lisa, *it was practice that made it perfect.*

Unit 8 Writing a discussion

Page 85

1 … homework helps students practise things they learn in class.

2 … children need to relax after school, not do more schoolwork.

3 … teachers mustn't give too much.

Page 86

Arguments for	Arguments against
a delicious treat	lots of sugar
good for parties	tooth decay
make us happy	can make us sick
make good presents	could spoil our appetite for healthier foods

Page 87

1 b, c, e, f 2 a lolly b party

3 will not

4 to show the appetites belong to the children

Pages 88–89

Step 1

1 C

2 Most children like chocolates and lollies. Some people think they should be allowed to eat them but others don't. There are arguments for and against on both sides.

Step 2

1 On the one hand 2 On the other hand

3 However 4 therefore

Step 3

b

Page 90

1 love

2 On the one hand, eating chocolates and lollies makes children happy.

In addition, birthday parties wouldn't be as much fun if children didn't have lollies to eat.

3 On the other hand

4 … they mustn't eat too many.

Page 91

Arguments for	Arguments against
television programs can be entertaining	some programs contain violence
can learn a lot from some programs	don't get any exercise watching television
children enjoy watching television	watching television could be bad for children's health
some programs are educational	many programs not suitable for children

Page 92

1 a, b, c, d, e

2 On the one hand, On the other hand, Also

3 arguments, violence, health

4 documentaries

Pages 93–94

Step 1

1 A

2 Most children like watching television. But is it a good thing for children to do? There are arguments for and against the idea.

Step 2

1 because 2 and 3 if 4 but 5 or

Step 3

1 b

2 Overall, I think that children should be allowed to watch television, as longs as they don't watch too much. They also shouldn't watch programs that contain bad language and violence.

3 **Suggestion**: Children also shouldn't watch programs that are rated M, and they should only watch programs rated PG if their parents say it is all right.

Page 95

Most children like watching television. But is it a good thing for children to do? There are arguments for and against this idea.

On the one hand, children enjoy watching television because many programs are entertaining. They make children happy. Lots of programs are also educational, like Frozen Planet. Children can learn a lot from them. If children watch the food programs, they can even learn how to cook.

On the other hand, many programs contain violence or bad language. These programs are not suitable for children. In addition, children who watch television all the time don't get enough exercise. This is bad for their health.

Overall, I think that children should be allowed to watch television, but they shouldn't watch too much. Also, they shouldn't be allowed to watch programs that have lots of violence and bad language in them.

Word bank

Unit 1 Writing a recount

Time connectives to link ideas:

after breakfast/lunch/dinner, afterwards, before, finally, first, first of all, in the morning/afternoon/evening, last of all, lastly, later, next, that morning/afternoon/night, the next morning/day, then

Adjectives that describe people, things and events:

amazing, astonishing, breathtaking, spectacular, stunning

big, enormous, huge, large

boring, dull, monotonous, uninteresting

colourful, bright, brilliant, vibrant

delicious, appetising, mouthwatering, tasty

amusing, entertaining, funny, hilarious

excellent, good, great, outstanding

Unit 2 Writing a description of an animal

Adjectives that describe animals:

bent, bowed, curved, rounded

adorable, beautiful, cute, delightful

enormous, gigantic, immense, massive

bulky, chunky, stocky, thick

coarse, fuzzy, rough, ruffled

short, stubby, stumpy

cuddly, lovable, snuggly, soft

powerful, strong, tough

Conjunctions to link phrases and clauses:

although, and, because, but, if, or, so, unless, until, when, while, yet

Unit 3 Writing a sound poem

Onomatopoeic words:

Animal sounds:

bees **buzz**

birds **twitter**

cats **meow**, **purr**

chicks **cheep**

cows **moo**

dogs **bark**, **growl**, **howl**, **whine**

donkeys **bray**

elephants **trumpet**

horses **neigh**, **whinny**

lions **roar**

mice **squeak**

monkeys **chatter**

parrots **squawk**

pigs **grunt**, **squeal**

sheep **baa**, **bleat**

turkeys **gobble**

Sounds people make:

Crying sounds: howl, squeal, whimper, whine, yowl

Eating and drinking sounds: burp, crunch, gulp, munch, slurp

Laughing sounds: chuckle, giggle

Shouting sounds: scream, screech, shriek

Talking sounds: babble, blabber, gasp, groan, grumble, jabber, moan, mumble, murmur, mutter, sigh, squabble, whisper

Sounds things make:

balloons **pop**

bells **clang, tinkle**

cameras and keyboards **click**

cars **zoom** by

clocks **tick**

doors **creak**

drains **gurgle**

fans **whirr**

knives and forks **clatter**

leaves **rustle**

the **pitter-patter** of raindrops

sausages **sizzle**

thunder **rumbles**

trains **rattle** by

water **splashes**

waves **crash**

Unit 4 Writing to persuade—expositions

Connectives to link arguments:

also, finally, first of all, firstly, for example, in addition, last of all, lastly, secondly

Conjunctions to link ideas:

although, and, because, but, if, or, so, unless, until, when, while, yet

Unit 5 Writing an information report

Scientific language:

This will depend on the subject you are writing about.

Deserts: arid, environment, oasis

Rainforests: canopy, deforestation, understorey

Reptiles: backbone, cold-blooded, scales

Solar system: asteroid, orbit, planet

Weather: Celsius, climate, temperature

Unit 6 Writing a procedure

Action verbs that might be useful in procedures:

apply	arrange	attach	cover
decorate	dip	fasten	finish
fix	rub	smooth	smear
spread	squeeze	tape	wipe

Adverbs to describe how something is done:

carefully	clearly	completely	diagonally
directly	evenly	exactly	firmly
gradually	immediately	lightly	regularly
safely	securely	thickly	tightly

Unit 7 Writing a narrative

Proverbs:

Every cloud has a silver lining. (Something good can come out of a bad situation.)

Don't count your chickens before they're hatched. (Don't rely on something before it happens.)

Practice make perfect. (The more you practise something, the better you get at it.)

You can't judge a book by its cover. (You can't tell what someone or something is like just by looking at them.)

The early bird catches the worm. (Act quickly if you want to be successful.)

Pride comes before a fall. (Don't be too full of confidence as something might happen to make you look foolish.)

Rome was not built in a day. (It takes time to do a job properly.)

You can lead a horse to water, but you can't make it drink. (You can give someone an opportunity, but you can't force them to take it.)

Figurative language—common sayings:

to be a couch potato (to not do much exercise)

to be full of beans (to be very energetic)

to be over the moon (to be very happy)

to catch red-handed (to catch someone while they are doing something wrong)

to feel off-colour (to feel ill)

to feel on top of the world (to be very happy)

to have a heart of gold (to be kind and generous)

to have butterflies in your stomach (to be nervous)

to jump out of your skin (to get a fright)

to let the cat out of the bag (to reveal a secret)

to look daggers at someone (to look angrily at someone)

to walk on air (to feel happy or excited)

Figurative language—similes:

as different as day and night

as dry as a bone

as regular as clockwork

as shiny as a new pin

as tough as leather

as warm as toast

to be packed like sardines

to grin like a Cheshire cat

to have a face like thunder

Descriptive verbs:

ask, beg, beseech, demand, implore, plead, request

bend, bow, crouch, stoop

hit, slam, smack, strike, whack

glance, glimpse, look, peek, peep, peer, scan, stare

complain, groan, moan, sob, whimper

prod, push, shove, thrust, jostle

announce, exclaim, mumble, murmur, say

beam, grin, smile

advise, command, inform, instruct, order, tell

hike, march, plod, stride, trudge, walk

Unit 8 Writing a discussion

Conjunctions:

although, and, because, but, if, or, so, unless, until, when, while

Connectives that show different ideas:

on the one hand	on the other hand
however	in contrast

Connectives that show order:

after that	finally	first	first of all
firstly	lastly	next	second
secondly	then		

Words to talk about ideas:

advantage	argument	disadvantage	issue
negative	opinion	positive	question
side	topic	view	viewpoint